Devil's Advocates

DEVIL'S ADVOCATES is a series of books devoted to exploring the classics of horror cinema. Contributors to the series come from the fields of teaching, academia, journalism and fiction, but all have one thing in common: a passion for the horror film and a desire to share it with the widest possible audience.

'The admirable Devil's Advocates series is not only essential – and fun – reading for the serious horror fan but should be set texts on any genre course.'
Dr Ian Hunter, Reader in Film Studies, De Montfort University, Leicester

'Auteur Publishing's new Devil's Advocates critiques on individual titles... offer bracingly fresh perspectives from passionate writers. The series will perfectly complement the BFI archive volumes.' **Christopher Fowler,** *Independent on Sunday*

'Devil's Advocates has proven itself more than capable of producing impassioned, intelligent analyses of genre cinema... quickly becoming the go-to guys for intelligent, easily digestible film criticism.' ***Horror Talk.com***

'Auteur Publishing continue the good work of giving serious critical attention to significant horror films.' *Black Static*

facebook DevilsAdvocatesbooks

DevilsAdBooks

Also available in this series

A Girl Walks Home Alone at Night Farshid Kazemi

Black Sunday Martyn Conterio

The Blair Witch Project Peter Turner

Blood and Black Lace Roberto Curti

The Blood on Satan's Claw David Evans-Powell

Candyman Jon Towlson

Cannibal Holocaust Calum Waddell

Cape Fear Rob Daniel

Carrie Neil Mitchell

The Company of Wolves James Gracey

The Conjuring Kevin J. Wetmore Jr.

Creepshow Simon Brown

Cruising Eugenio Ercolani & Marcus Stiglegger

The Curse of Frankenstein Marcus K. Harmes

Daughters of Darkness Kat Ellinger

Dead of Night Jez Conolly & David Bates

The Descent James Marriot

The Devils Darren Arnold

Don't Look Now Jessica Gildersleeve

The Evil Dead Lloyd Haynes

The Fly Emma Westwood

Frenzy Ian Cooper

Halloween Murray Leeder

House of Usher Evert Jan van Leeuwen

In the Mouth of Madness Michael Blyth

It Follows Joshua Grimm

Ju-on The Grudge Marisa Hayes

Let the Right One In Anne Billson

M Samm Deighan

Macbeth Rebekah Owens

The Mummy Doris V. Sutherland

Nosferatu Cristina Massaccesi

Peeping Tom Kiri Bloom Walden

Prevenge Andrew Graves

Re-Animator Eddie Falvey

Repulsion Jeremy Carr

Saw Benjamin Poole

Scream Steven West

Scrooge Colin Fleming

The Shining Laura Mee

Shivers Luke Aspell

The Silence of the Lambs Barry Forshaw

Suspiria Alexandra Heller-Nicholas

The Texas Chain Saw Massacre James Rose

The Thing Jez Conolly

Trouble Every Day Kate Robertson

Twin Peaks: Fire Walk With Me Lindsay Hallam

Witchfinder General Ian Cooper

Forthcoming

[REC] Jim Harper

Dawn of the Dead Jon Towlson

The Omen Adrian Schober

Snuff Mark McKenna

Devil's Advocates

Possession

Alison Taylor

Acknowledgements

I am first and foremost grateful to the kindness and generosity of Daniel Bird. Any research into Żuławski is indebted to Bird at a fundamental level, and it is upon the foundations of his research that this book is built. Beyond this, Bird provided me with guidance and materials that have helped make this book possible. I would also like to extend my warmest gratitude to Sam Neill for taking the time to offer his reflections on this incredible film, and to Marie-Laure Reyre who generously permitted me to reproduce archival materials from *Possession*'s pre-production and production phases. To the ever patient and kind John Atkinson, thank you for your enduring support. Thank you also to the BBFC.

So many people have been integral to this book, both personally and professionally. Some of you helped me track down leads, trekked around Berlin with me, let me use your library log-in, provided me with incredible resources, or allowed me to pick your brain. Others were steadfast sounding boards and encouraging voices. Many were both. A big thank you to: Ariel Baska, Andreas Berg, Shuktika Bose, Evette Braunstein, Daniel Brennan, Joseph Clowes, Thomas Coghlan, Eleanor Colla, Sally Cooper, Michelle Dicinoski, John Edmond, Chris Fitchett, Buddy Giovinazzo, Michael Goddard, Caroline Graham, Alexandra Heller-Nicholas, Jason Jacobs, Kier-La Janisse, Scott Knight, Rebecca McKenzie, Katarina Needham, Rachel Peate, Liesl Pfeffer, Jason Reed, Margot Johnston, Justine Peres Smith, Zoë Rose Smith, Valerie Spall, Deborah Thomas, Kate Warner, Daniel Walker, Marcin Wierzchosławski, and of course, my family.

First published in 2022 by
Auteur, an imprint of
Liverpool University Press,
4 Cambridge Street,
Liverpool
L69 7ZU

Series design: Nikki Hamlett at Cassels Design
Set by Cassels Design, Luton UK

All rights reserved. No part of this publication may be reproduced in any material form (including photocopying or storing in any medium by electronic means and whether or not transiently or incidentally to some other use of this publication) without the permission of the copyright owner.

All illustrations from *Possession* © Gaumont/Oliane Productions/Marianne Productions. Others are as indicated in the picture caption.

British Library Cataloguing-in-Publication Data
A catalogue record for this book is available from the British Library

ISBN paperback: 978-1-80085-706-3
ISBN hardback: 978-1-80085-705-6
ISBN epub: 978-1-80085-831-2
ISBN PDF: 978-1-80085-749-0

Contents

Chapter 1: Faith and Chance 7

Chapter 2: 'It's about a woman who fucks with an octopus' 23

Chapter 3: Up the spiral staircase 49

Chapter 4: 'If you had only seen what I saw!' – *Possession*'s Reception 81

Chapter 5: 'Does our subject still wear pink socks?' – *Possession*'s Legacy 95

Bibliography 110

To C. – what good fortune.

Chapter 1: Faith and Chance

There really is no other film quite like *Possession* (1981). Those who have heard of, but haven't yet experienced it, may be aware of its most notorious scene. Anna, played by France's pixie-faced film darling Isabelle Adjani, taken with maniacal laughter charges wide eyed into an empty Berlin U-Bahn tunnel. As Anna twirls and crashes into the subway walls, laughter becomes scream and her already strange physicality escalates into inhuman frenzy. She smashes her grocery bag against the tiles, causing what might be milk to ejaculate forcefully, painting the walls and her already dishevelled blue dress with white muck. Now shrieking, she doubles over and whips back upright. Her palms opened outwards are raised to her face and her shrieks descend into rhythmic grunts, surely on the verge of hyperventilation. The air seems to pull at her; Anna's body is besieged by violent jerks that evolve into shamanic dance. The arms, no longer hers, expel and retract, the body contorts and spins, fierce spasms agitate as though Anna is caught in a tug of war by contending forces unseen. It's a dizzying and grotesque display. Thrust to the ground, Anna rolls in filth. In the scene's climax Anna kneels, legs splayed, fists clenched painfully between her thighs. The mouth gasps and screams, a white fluid draining from it down her chin. From her shoulders and vagina more pale fluid oozes, combined with blood. Face bent upward to the heavens, eyes open wide, she gasps violently for breath, before her whole form constricts to hold it in, causing the eyes to bulge. A strangled silence gives way to a tremendous scream. The scene ends abruptly.

I will admit to having felt haunted by *Possession* ever since I first saw it. I recall being awestruck and terrified by this moment in the U-Bahn; never before had I seen an actor give so much of themselves. Adjani's performance is so overwhelmingly unguarded it looks as though it is happening to her—an involuntary convulsion, rather than willed movement. So completely given over to this unrestrained physicality, it seems she may very well crack her skull on the wall and not notice. She has gone brilliantly, exquisitely mad, and it feels contagious.

In this way, *Possession* is not a film that affords a safe, critical distance. It is possible, of course, to reject *Possession* as outlandish and gruesome—many have. To take it seriously is to embrace its eccentricities and extremes and surrender oneself to the physical and psychic deterioration of its characters. Writing for *Le Figaro*, François Chalais articulates the invitation *Possession* offers: "One enters, or one does not enter, this film. And I pity those who refuse to cross the threshold, those who feel comfortable" (qtd. in Fortier 1981: 39). If Andrzej Żuławski invites us across the threshold, this book aims to be a guide for what lurks on the other side.

Possession is a strange object, difficult to pin down because it is so many things. A piece of auteur cinema from a filmmaker largely ignored throughout his career. A genre film that has the iconography of lowbrow fare like creature features and spy thrillers while not really fulfilling the expectations of either. A depiction of a marital breakdown which is at once brutally honest and utterly absurd. A film that gestures towards an internal coherence replete with nightmarish symbols and metaphors, but which ultimately eludes apprehension. A highbrow art film which premiered in competition at the Cannes Film Festival, only to be temporarily outlawed in the UK as a work of obscenity. As long-time collaborator of Żuławski, Daniel Bird states: "The virtue of *Possession* is that it cannot be reduced to something manageable or comfortable, it cannot be tamed or categorised" (Bird 2003b: 369). *Possession* is more vital than any single category can hold, its status and meanings shifting over time.

I've long wanted to write about *Possession* but have always come up hesitant. How to write a book about a work that seems to change shape like the monster it depicts? While its strangeness is seductive, its convoluted plot makes it an intimidating object when faced with the task of trying to put its mysteries and pleasures into words. I know I'm not alone in feeling daunted. Reviewing the film in 1981, Max Tessier stated that "it would be futile, or even absurd, to attempt a summary of the movie or an overview of its plot" (1981a: 19). As one will garner from the following synopsis, itself not exhaustive, *Possession* is an unwieldy film.

Synopsis

Possession tells the story of a marital breakdown in Cold War era Berlin. Marc (Sam Neill) returns to his wife, Anna (Isabelle Adjani) and child, Bob (Michael Hogben) in the West after a year on the other side of the Wall carrying out an undisclosed espionage mission. Having completed his contract, Marc meets with his employers, a mysterious panel of men in suits, to announce his resignation for family reasons. Despite their protestations, Marc remains firm, stating they should hire his successor. When Marc returns from this meeting, Anna is gone. Searching the apartment for clues as to his wife's whereabouts, Marc discovers evidence of Anna's infidelity, and the pair agree to meet at Café Einstein to negotiate their future, but this rendezvous quickly turns volatile. In the following scene, Marc appears to be having a nervous breakdown in a hotel room, from which he emerges three weeks later.

Returning to the family apartment, Marc discovers Bob has been left alone for some time. After another heated argument upon Anna's arrival, Marc comforts her and the pair fall asleep. Marc is awoken by the telephone, a male voice informing him that "Anna is with me, and she'll stay with me." Dropping Bob at school the following day, Marc is shocked to discover his son's teacher, Helen (also Adjani) bears a perfect resemblance to Anna save for her green eyes and light brown fringe hairstyle. Helen, and Anna's friend, Margie (Margit Carstensen) will become surrogate carers for Bob while Marc is preoccupied, trying to win back the affections of his elusive wife who continues to disappear from the apartment for days at a time.

Marc tracks Anna's lover, a ludicrous guru figure named Heinrich (Heinz Bennent) to the apartment he shares with his elderly mother. The fight that ensues reveals that Anna's absences from home cannot be explained as visits to Heinrich, and Marc seeks the help of a private investigator who tails her to a bare apartment in Kreuzberg. Inside, Anna harbours her real secret—a phallic and slimy tentacled creature that is also her lover. Anna murders those who she perceives as threats to its discovery, starting with the private investigator whom she stabs in the throat with a broken bottle.

Also disturbed by Anna's absence, Heinrich attempts to visit her at the family apartment. Revealing she no longer resides there, Marc relishes Heinrich's anguish at discovering that he too is subject to Anna's infidelity. Helping care for Bob at the family apartment, Helen raises her concerns about the boy's strange behaviour at school. Marc confides his own troubles and the pair grow intimate. The following day, another private detective, Zimmerman, approaches Marc with his concerns about his colleague (and romantic partner) who failed to return after following Anna. Upon receiving the Kreuzberg address, Zimmerman too will be murdered by Anna.

Marc discovers a package left for him by Heinrich, containing a home movie. In it, Anna agitatedly tries to explain her feelings in a cryptic monologue about two sisters: faith and chance. More erratic and tormented than ever, Anna returns to the family apartment, and her attempt to explain her emotions to Marc prompts a flashback. Here we see Anna in a church, moaning while gazing up at an icon of Christ crucified, before entering the U-Bahn and having a gruesome miscarriage. Having heard Anna's—albeit bizarre—explanation, Marc seems to better understand what she is going through. Again, Anna leaves abruptly.

Heinrich finds Anna at the Kreuzberg apartment, attempting to seduce her before discovering the monster, and the dismembered bodies of her prior victims. Anna wounds Heinrich and he flees the apartment to telephone Marc for help. Marc has begun following his wife into madness, however, and finding the Kreuzberg apartment empty, he destroys it to cover up her crimes. Marc then meets Heinrich in the men's room of a local bar, killing him after Heinrich attempts blackmail. Returning home, Marc discovers another of Anna's victims—Margie collapses into his arms, her throat slashed. Hiding her body in the apartment, Marc and Anna make love before executing a plan to tie up any loose ends and escape.

That night, Marc drops Bob at Helen's, and goes to meet Anna, only to find her in bed having sex with the tentacle monster. Disturbed and fascinated, Marc stares awestruck, Anna desperately repeating "almost" as the now human-tentacle hybrid writhes over her. He then visits Heinrich's mother who has called for him, concerned that while Heinrich's body has been discovered, his soul is nowhere to be found. After lamenting the loss of her son, she takes some pills and lays down in bed, presumably to die.

The following day Marc is met by one of his former employers, who tries again to convince him to continue with their mission. When he pulls up to Margie's home where Anna is hiding, Marc observes another member of this shadowy organization working with police, and wages an attack on them only to be injured in the ensuing shoot out, before managing to escape. In the film's grisly climax, Marc, severely injured in a motorcycle accident, climbs a spiral staircase. Anna finds him collapsed on the stairs, proudly presenting the fully metamorphosed creature—a perfect replica of her husband. Pursued by Marc's former employers, Anna is injured, before taking Marc's gun and shooting both herself and Marc simultaneously. The creature, immune to gunfire escapes, and goes to Helen's apartment. Bob cautions Helen not to open the door, but when Helen dismisses his concerns, the child runs and dives face-first into the bathtub, perhaps to drown himself. With the creature's silhouette waiting to enter, we hear the sound of bomber planes and sirens as the lighting flickers, signalling the apocalypse.

ORIGINS

> This film comes from a very simple vision: we are all unhappy, and we don't deserve it. – Andrzej Żuławski (2000)

At its most simple, *Possession* is the story of a marital breakdown. But this breakdown is rendered in the most far-flung and expressionist terms. The pain and anguish of love torn asunder, and the extreme emotions such an experience carries are violently literalised on screen. If one has ever felt the suffering of love lost as world ending, they will understand why Żuławski needs an apocalypse to convey it. *Possession*'s performances are beyond histrionic, its situations more than absurd. Language seems incapable of capturing the extremes to which Żuławski pushes his material. As Charles Bluhdorn of Paramount Pictures said when Żuławski pitched the idea to him: "This is impossible!" Żuławski replied: "Yes, it is impossible, but it's possible in certain circumstances. In certain places. In a certain state of mind" (Żuławski 2000). The circumstances would be a combination of faith and chance. The place would be a divided Berlin. And that state of mind, for Żuławski, was conjured from a series of devastating life events.

Żuławski studied direction in Paris, completing a thesis on Andrzej Wajda's second feature *Kanal* (1957), the harrowing story of young resistance fighters in the Warsaw uprising of 1944. Returning to Poland, Żuławski apprenticed under Wajda who would grow to be one of Poland's premiere filmmakers. While Wajda's early films, several upon which Żuławski would serve as second unit director, are far more stylistically restrained than his protégé's, his influence is palpable from the outset. Żuławski's first feature, a scathing and surreal depiction of German-occupied Poland, *The Third Part of the Night* (1971) pays direct homage to Wajda's first feature *A Generation* (1955). Echoing a scene in Wajda's film in which a young resistance fighter is pursued by Germans up an open well spiral staircase, Żuławski's protagonist in *The Third Part of the Night* narrowly escapes death when Germans chase him up a staircase only to kill a similarly dressed man by mistake.

A Generation *(Wajda 1955)* © *Studio Filmowe Kadr.*

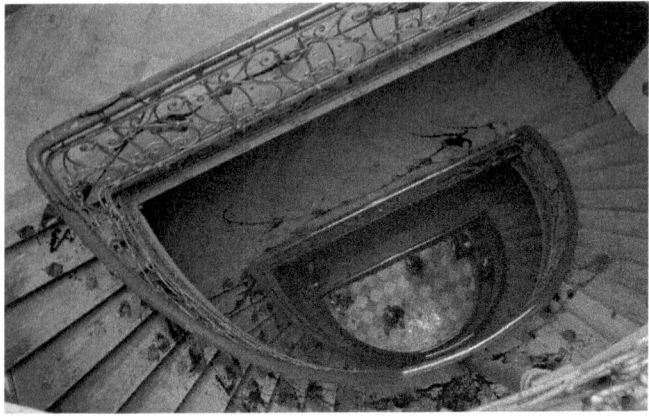

Possession *(Żuławski 1981).*

While in Wajda's films, the German occupation of Poland provides the backdrop for tales of youthful optimism and collective struggle, for Żuławski this subject matter becomes the stuff of hallucinatory nightmare. *The Third Part of the Night* opens with a reading from the Book of Revelation, a text which seems to summon the hell it prophesizes. Michal (Leszek Teleszyński), disoriented after recuperating from a severe illness, awakens to find his wife, Helena (Małgorzata Braunek), reading the Bible to him. Sending him and their young son for a walk in the surrounding woodlands, Helena and Michal's mother are ambushed moments later when German soldiers on horseback storm the house. Distracted, Michal does not notice that his son has strayed. A gunshot sounds and a frenetic hand-held camera races alongside Michal as he frantically makes his way through the trees. In a horrific moment of recognition, the film cuts between Helena's terror-stricken and bloody face, and her perspective: her child running from the woods towards certain death. Michal, though still distant, is close enough to witness the slaughter of his family. Combined with Andrzej Korzyński's experimental score—an agitating combination of strings, low drone electric guitar and booming percussion—the scene is truly nightmarish. Already surreal, violent, and apocalyptic, Żuławski's first feature looks towards *Possession*, and the resonances only grow as the film continues. Korzyński's score, a family wrenched apart, the dizzyingly mobile camera, a bloody shootout on a spiral staircase, and characters who find their uncanny echo in doubles reveal Żuławski's preoccupations for decades to come.

Żuławski's second feature, *The Devil* (1972) likewise deals with the invasion of Poland, this time by the Prussian army in the late eighteenth century. Even more hellish than its predecessor, *The Devil* follows Jakub (Teleszyński) a political prisoner emancipated by a mysterious stranger (Wojciech Pszoniak) and sent home to discover the life he knew has been devastated in his absence. Presuming him dead, his fiancée (Braunek) is now pregnant to a former friend turned state collaborator, his father has committed suicide, his sister has gone mad, and the mother who abandoned him as a child is now the madam of a nearby brothel. The stranger, a "lowly clerk" and devil of the film's title, guides Jakub like a puppet master, parading him from horror to horror. "Go and see!" the devil proclaims with glee before sending him into his mother's bordello, making the film's apocalyptic resonance explicit.

In *The Devil* too we see the seeds of *Possession*. Even more than in Żuławski's prior film, the camera charges, shudders, and spins, wrapping one up in the frenzy of its characters. Braunek's hyperbolic performance as Narzeczona meshes the erotic and hysterical, as will Adjani's Anna almost a decade later. The film is also punctuated by bursts of bloody violence, the stranger/devil always appearing right when Jakub's emotions hit fever pitch to hand him a straight razor.

Despite being produced by Wajda's film company, both *The Third Part of the Night* and *The Devil* were radically different in style from dominant tendencies in post-war Polish cinema. Żuławski's formal experimentation set him apart from the neorealist aesthetics of the 'Polish School' filmmakers of the 1950s and early 1960s, and the realism of the 'Cinema of Moral Concern' that came to the fore in the late 1970s. The latter tendency produced films about contemporary Polish life, which afforded filmmakers opportunity to make veiled criticisms of communist Poland, though the limitations of state censorship ensured any political engagement was so generalised as to be implicit (Goddard 2014: 242). Referring to the Cinema of Moral Concern, Michael Goddard notes, "For Żuławski cinematic politics and aesthetics are inseparable, and it is hard to imagine anyone more at odds with this prevailing tendency" (Goddard 2014: 242). Rather, Goddard (2012) argues Żuławski had more in common with Walerian Borowczyk, Roman Polanski, and Jerzy Skolimowski whose careers were similarly marred by censorship, marginalisation, and exile.

Moreover, Żuławski's early Polish films lay the ground for other tensions which will prove crucial to *Possession*'s creation, starting with his marriage to star Małgorzata Braunek. In interviews, Żuławski has been upfront about the collapse of his marriage being the inspiration for *Possession*, a film he considers autobiographical (Żuławski 2000). Between the screams of its protagonists, who seem driven by such frenzied desperation that they might tear each other to pieces, is a supreme anguish and vulnerability. Dialogue between Marc and Anna, performed with unchecked animosity, is, according to Żuławski, recollected from real arguments, the detritus of a painful divorce ruptured in part by Braunek's infidelity. It is this relatively ordinary premise that gives the film its human anchor. For all its excesses, its madness and monster, its blood and gore, *Possession* brings us close, uncomfortably so, to a core aspect of human experience.

The bitterness of heartbreak is one aspect of *Possession*'s enmity; the director's run-ins with Polish censors, beginning with *The Devil*, is another. Żuławski's tale of a disillusioned young man corrupted by a Government puppet master into murdering everyone around him was a political criticism not lost on authorities despite its being cloaked in eighteenth-century garb. When the Minister of Culture saw the film, it was immediately banned and would remain so until 1987 (Bird 2003a: 148). This would only be the beginning of Żuławski's trouble with an oppressive communist regime, however. The truly devastating blow to the director's freedom of expression at the hands of the Ministry of Culture would come some years later, when he returned to Poland after a period of exile in France.

Following the success and critical acclaim of his French production, *The Important Thing is to Love* (1975), Żuławski was able to return to Poland to attempt the most ambitious project of his entire career: a science fiction epic adapted from his uncle, Jerzy Żuławski's Lunar Trilogy. Finally released in 1988, *On the Silver Globe* is an enormous and expensive undertaking about a trio of scientists who begin a new colony on the moon, after their ship crash lands. The plot weaves a vast and convoluted rumination on religion, existentialism, and humanity, complete with bloody battles against a species of monstrous birds, cave orgies, and grotesque seaside crucifixions. In order to translate Żuławski's vision, scores of performers in elaborate tribal costumes were assembled in the Gobi Desert creating the film's otherworldly setting. Performances and film style are uniformly hyperbolic: characters scream their lines, the camera swooping towards them or crane-mounted to capture enormous congregations on the Baltic coastline. *On the Silver Globe* is both grandiose and unprecedented; as David Thompson (2007: 90) described it, Żuławski's film is "perhaps akin to Tarkovsky on acid."

That we are able to see this film at all is somewhat miraculous. While Żuławski's script had already received the approval of the Ministry of Culture and production was well under way, the appointment of Janusz Wilhelmi as the Deputy Minister of Culture and Art saw the film stopped in its tracks approximately two-thirds of the way through shooting. In spite of the time and expense already spent on the film, in an extraordinary flex of power, the State froze production and ordered all sets and costumes be destroyed (Bird 2003a: 148; Mishałek & Turaj 1988: 57). Thankfully, some materials were preserved clandestinely by dedicated cast and crew. Żuławski would 'complete' the film several years later, stitching together the footage shot with new imagery of himself walking around contemporary Warsaw narrating the missing scenes. This version of the film, part extraordinary formal experiment, part forlorn testament to the personal loss incurred under an oppressive communist regime, would at last premiere at Cannes in 1988.

While in retrospect, the survival of *On the Silver Globe* in any form is a positive, the devastation the Ministry's actions wrought on Żuławski cannot be overstated. As the director reflected on this tumultuous period in a 2009 interview: "The simple basis of [*Possession*] was my private life, which just exploded. Not only the film, the science fiction film was stopped, but I had no home, no family; my wife, the mother of my son went away with a guy like Heinrich" (Bird 2009a). If the monster that Anna miscarries in the U-Bahn is the product of the psychic trauma sparked by desire, anguish, and the otherwise unresolvable struggle between competing identities and impulses, then *Possession* is Żuławski's monster, conjured of anger and heartbreak, violently expelled into a world not ready.

Horror

Żuławski's cinema spans a range of genres from science fiction to opera, though here the term genre is more accurately a loose but handy approximation, as his films hardly conform to expectations. For Żuławski, genre cinema is a "mask" beneath which one might conceal one's motive and advance ideas (Bird 2009a). While it is not unusual for genre films to provide the means for social commentary, within the confines of communist Poland, the disguise of genre has higher stakes. *On the Silver Globe* adopted the mask of science fiction (though sadly authorities saw through it) in order to launch a profound critique of religion, dogma, and human nature. *Possession*, made outside of the bounds of Poland, employed the horror genre, this time to critique the political and familial structures that had rejected its author.

Possession poster art by Basha Baranowska. Courtesy of Oliane Productions.

Historically, horror and other fantastic genres have made up very little of Poland's film output, which has a sustained emphasis on realist films. Ewa Mazierska (2007: 16-17) attributes this lack to both an industrial reluctance to compete with Hollywood in genres that require spectacle, and a cultural sense of duty to depict the present. Amid this scarcity, however, rest some notable examples, and so Żuławski's early features stand apart, rather than alone in this sense. In exquisite black and white compositions, Jerzy Kawalerowicz's *Mother Joan of the Angels* (1961) depicts a seventeenth-century convent, its abbess allegedly possessed by demons. Save for an axe murder that occurs offscreen in the film's climax, horror elements remain implicit, signalled through agitated performances rather than supernatural spectacle. In contrast, Wojciech Has's big budget fantastical epic, *The Saragossa Manuscript* (1965) is uncharacteristically grandiose in its visuals, an ambitious realisation of Jan Potocki's kaleidoscopic narrative interweaving several supernatural tales. Later, Has's formal experimentation would be pushed even further with the dreamlike logic of *The Hourglass Sanitorium* (1973), its protagonist stumbling through elaborately choreographed settings incongruent in space and time. More restrained, Janusz Majewski's *Lokis: A Manuscript of Professor Wittembach* (1970) almost eschews the spectacle of horror altogether, inspiring dread via its Gothic setting and Wojciech Kilar's haunting score. Beyond the Iron Curtain, other Polish émigrés made significant contributions to the horror canon. Roman Polanski's *Repulsion* (1965) is a claustrophobic rumination on sexual repression, as its young heroine descends into madness in her London apartment. Striking expressionist visuals, including a hallway enlivened with scores of groping hands, uncomfortably align us with Carol's (Catherine Deneuve) psychic deterioration. Three years later, Polanski's stylistically subdued but no less unnerving American production, *Rosemary's Baby* (1968) would horrify audiences for the first time. Meanwhile, Walerian Borowczyk was taking advantage of France's permissive film culture, launching his erotic-horror hybrids, including the scandalously explicit *The Beast* (1975) and his visually sumptuous *The Strange Case of Dr. Jekyll and Miss Osbourne* (1981).

Horror affords opportunities for stylistic experimentation in the way that few other genres do. Even so, the transition between the 1970s to the 1980s saw the arrival of some of the genre's most significant and strange entries. Dario Argento's lavish and sensual *Suspiria* (1977), Nobuhiko Ôbayashi's hysterical and hallucinatory *House* (1977), David Lynch's surreal *Eraserhead* (1977) and Stanley Kubrick's enigmatic *The Shining* (1980) are all typified by stylistic innovation. With its pallid blue colour palette, restless wide-angle camera, and frenzied performances, *Possession* is no less remarkable.

Like these other extraordinary films, *Possession* is hardly a straight horror film. While its monster, doppelgängers, and grisly murders suggest its allegiance to the genre, much of its unsettling effect can be attributed to the emotional extremes of a couple in conflict. *Possession*'s monster may strike Heinrich temporarily blind, but to viewers it's more of a grotesque curiosity, posing a threat only to Marc and Anna's marriage. Anna's bursts of homicidal violence are indeed gruesome, and there is a generic reveal when Heinrich spies dismembered body parts in her refrigerator, however, the film's real anxiety and dread is evinced in the fraught exchanges between a couple unhinged. Claustrophobic camerawork suffocates Marc and Anna in their most vulnerable moments. The extremities of performance confront us with the ungovernable violence of impassioned human suffering. And like Polanski, Żuławski finds the domestic world to be the true locus of horror. Moreover, the 'possession' of the film's title is not the demonic kind that the uninitiated viewer might expect. Despite the film's abundant references to biblical good and evil, its characters are not beset by malignant spirits. Rather, possession, in Żuławski's vision is the will to possess the other. It is at once possession in the public sense: the control of an oppressive State that would erect an enormous barrier to possess its citizens by deadly force. Simultaneously, it is possession in the private sense of human intimacy: that clawing, desperate, all-consuming, and destructive drive to master another.

While *Possession* is hardly a straight horror film, it is, of course, not completely out of the realm of the genre either. Korzyński's use of shivering strings, droning synth and piercingly high flute in the film's opening set the nerves on edge right from the outset. The film's tone is unsettling; its situations inspire dread and at times, revulsion. Marc's attempts to understand Anna's distress evoke a Lovecraftian 'cosmic horror'—not in the sense of alien or supernatural forces, but in the sense that an encounter with that which is beyond comprehension is liable to drive one mad. Remarkably, though, the incomprehensible 'evil' is decidedly human. It is a deteriorating marriage in a city divided by ideology. These are not the aberrations of an otherworldly realm; these are the evils borne of banality.

STRUCTURE

The remainder of this book offers an examination of *Possession*, from its pre-production through to its legacy. That *Possession* is the film it is, and not some other film—produced by, and starring others—is the result of faith and chance. Of course, *Possession* is Żuławski's film, but if not for the various talents, happy and not-so-happy accidents, the finished product might have looked very different. Considering the pre-production and production process, the next chapter examines the various decisions and contingencies that came together allowing Żuławski to birth this beautiful monster. From the director's harmonious collaboration with author Frederic Tuten, to a very fraught and at times dangerous on-set atmosphere, to a directorial method with its origins in Haitian voodoo trance-states, Chapter 2 is concerned with how the film we know came to be.

Chapter 3 ventures up the spiral staircase, engaging in a critical analysis of the film by considering its themes, structure, and style. While *Possession* is resistant to any singular interpretation, better experienced than 'explained,' this chapter endeavours to explore key moments and motifs to enrich our appreciation. I take as a guide the pattern of the winding staircase, a recurring motif across Żuławski's films, which the director held to have spiritual significance as a passage between worlds. Via its serpentine architecture, the spiral staircase provides an insight into the way Żuławski patterns his exploration of division and duality, the private and political.

Chapter 4 grapples with *Possession*'s polarising reception. The film's resistance to tidy categorisation would only be exacerbated upon its release where it would occupy an uncertain position between arthouse and grindhouse. As Joan Hawkins notes of de Sade's writings being simultaneously housed in university libraries and sold in sex shops (1999: 17), *Possession* likewise held the paradoxical position of being showcased at the world's leading art cinema festival in competition for the illustrious Palme d'Or, and being maligned as exploitation. At Cannes, the film was both lauded and loathed. In Britain, the film was banned as obscene. And between these Jekyll and Hyde extremes, was the truly monstrous United States release: a Frankensteinian re-edit borne of a lax deal with international distributors.

Like so many great works, *Possession* was by and large misunderstood upon its release. However, in the decades since its scandals and legal complications, the film has found an audience, gradually developing a cult following. As Chapter 5 will explore, Żuławski's monster lives on, not only in loving restorations and retrospectives, but in a new generation of filmmakers who cite the film as an influence. Even forty years after its initial release, the film's power has not dissipated; beyond its visceral power to shock and disturb, *Possession* has also garnered a feminist appreciation for its potent exploration of female experience. This final chapter reflects on *Possession* today—its legacy, influence, and its long overdue recognition as a significant work of art.

This is necessarily an incomplete story. While I've assembled the pieces I could find, it's clear that much remains hidden. The reluctance for those involved with the film to tell a complete story is not unusual; for whatever reason, there appear to be areas that, even after the passing of its director, and four decades after its release, are too delicate to broach and so several lacunae remain. Rather than fill these gaps with speculation, I have opted to note them when they arise.

I will take the liberty of presuming anyone reading the following chapters has seen the film. I will also be forthright in saying that this book does not claim to be a comprehensive explanation of *Possession*. As with other great works of enigmatic cinema, to offer up a singular or definitive reading would be reductive. Rather, I feel the best a guide can hope to do is furnish the context of the film's creation and bring into conversation some of its unruly tendrils, that we might better appreciate it. Just as Kubrick's *The Shining* invites us to the surrender to the paradoxical logic of The Overlook Hotel, I think *Possession* is best approached like the winding staircase in the film's climax: a work of beautiful if complicated symmetry, a passage between spaces, designed at once to facilitate and hinder one's ascent.

Chapter 2: 'It's About a Woman Who Fucks With an Octopus'

Perhaps my favourite anecdote about *Possession* is Żuławski's recollection of pitching it to the founder of Gulf & Western, and head of Paramount Pictures, Charlie Bluhdorn. The story, as Żuławski tells it, happened over dinner. One can imagine the oddness of this dynamic, a self-made corporate powerhouse sat opposite the charismatic young director, a self-proclaimed bastion of "poor man's cinema."

"What's your next film?" Bluhdorn asked.
"Possession."
"Well, what is it about?"
"Listen, it's about a woman who fucks with an octopus."
[Bluhdorn apparently looked at Żuławski as though he had lost his mind. But moments later, Bluhdorn was sold.]
"Ok. How much money do you need?"
"We need like, I don't know, 2 million dollars..."
"You have it! Do it!" (Żuławski 2000)

Żuławski would do it. But, of course, *Possession*'s production would not be so simple. While the French arm of Paramount would co-finance the film, there would be plenty of obstacles before Żuławski's monster could come to life. Between a disappearing producer, an onset altercation resolved with a death threat, a traumatized lead, and drunken stunt doubles hell-bent on doing as much self-harm as possible, the film's production history is almost as bizarre as the finished product. That's what this chapter is about.

It must be said that reconstructing *Possession* as an outsider feels a little like trying to piece together the timeline in a criminal investigation long after the fact. Much of the information that exists surrounding the pre-production and production phases of *Possession* is anecdotal, so must be taken with a grain of salt. One can sift through the testimony of witnesses in an attempt to assemble something like a composite sketch of what happened, but memories are flawed, motives conflict, and some voices are louder than others. When assembling the narratives of those who have spoken, one also gets the sense that there is wide spectrum of players; for some, sincerity is matched by diplomacy, the recollection of a difficult moment retreating into strategic vagueness. Others seem to refuse to let the truth get in the way of a good yarn. At this latter end of the spectrum is Dominique Schneidre's weaving of memoir and fiction, *Trois verres de vodka* (2017). There is no doubt that Schneidre had a good insight into Żuławski during this period; it was at Schneidre's home in St. Tropez that much of *Possession*'s screenplay was written. Yet, as *roman à clef*, we cannot regard it as fact, even if we suspect that some of its outlandish claims likely still contain an element of truth. Ultimately, there is much we still don't know. For instance, after describing his collaboration with Żuławski on the screenplay, co-writer Frederic Tuten laughs in interview with Milly Iatrou: "That's the abridged version of my relationship to *Possession*. It's very abridged. The truth will come out one day after I'm dead" (Tuten qtd. in Iatrou & Morgan 2019).

Pre-production advertisement published in Variety *May 9, 1979. Courtesy of Oliane Productions.*

Pre-Production

As discussed in the previous chapter, *Possession* is a monster spawned of Żuławski's personal and professional angst in the wake of a deteriorating marriage and the termination of *On the Silver Globe* at the hands of Polish censors. Żuławski says the idea for *Possession* arose while in Warsaw, the story to unfold against a backdrop of socialism

(Bonitzer & Toubiana 1981: 43). After his science fiction epic was shut down, however, Żuławski was prohibited from working in Poland, and so *Possession* would have to be made elsewhere. Christian Ferry, then president of Paramount's French subsidiary, invited Żuławski to New York, ostensibly to do urgent work on a film. Żuławski explains the offer was fictious, but the money was real, and was enough to secure Żuławski a passport from the crumbling communist regime: "I was told 'You have 24 hours to leave the country quietly. Let's see what you say in the West'" (Żuławski qtd. in Wybon 2009). Alone in a New York hotel room, Żuławski sat with a typewriter and a lot of whiskey and began drafting *Possession* (Bonitzer & Toubiana 1981: 43).

What Żuławski would have to say in the West was as politically incendiary as his Polish works; Żuławski has described his vision for *Possession* as a "totally anti-Marxian narrative against a background of Marxism" (Bonitzer & Toubiana 1981: 43). What better backdrop than the concrete border of the Eastern bloc? For Żuławski the Wall that divided East and West made Berlin the ideal place to set his latest critique of the communist system. The Wall's symbolic resonance was immense, the material manifestation of an ideological schism.

Possession was to be an English-language feature, intended to target a wider audience than a Polish- or French-language film (Żuławski 2000). Żuławski approached Danièle Thompson to collaborate on the screenplay. Thompson declined (though the pair would later collaborate on *Malady of Love* [Deray 1987]), instead recommending a partnership with American novelist and film critic, Frederic Tuten. Intrigued by Żuławski's idea, Tuten agreed, and the pair set to work. Tuten recalls the working relationship as a positive one; Żuławski's preparation and professionalism were impressive, and the pair never came to any serious blows (Bird 2009a).

Originally attached to produce the film was Pierre Caro, who had worked on films including Jacques Deray's *Borsalino* (1970) and Robert Enrico's *The Old Gun* (1975). This arrangement would come to a sudden halt, however. Tuten recalls receiving a call from Żuławski informing him the producer was bankrupt: "I'm laughing because the last time I had lunch with Pierre Caro in Paris, he said to me 'oh Fred, can I borrow 500 Francs?'...I thought, this is a bad sign" (qtd. in Iatrou & Morgan 2019). Żuławski had been staying in a New York hotel when Caro phoned to inform him there were no funds to cover the bill. Caro had not only gone bankrupt but had left France; Tuten describes this moment: "he literally, truly disappeared" (Bird 2009a). This event would stall pre-production until 1978. Volunteering to cover the debts Caro had abandoned was Marie-Laure Reyre, an early-career producer. With Reyre at the helm, pre-production could progress.

CAST

Possession could easily have been a different film with a different cast. As late as a month before shooting would commence, pre-production advertising billed a completely different male line up including Chris Sarandon of *Dog Day Afternoon* (1975), Helmut Griem of *Cabaret* (1972), and Sterling Hayden of Kubrick's *The Killing* (1956) and *Dr. Strangelove* (1964) (*Variety* 1980: 33). Presumably Sarandon, Griem, and Hayden would play Marc, Heinrich, and Abe (a character who would later be cut) respectively. Originally, Sam Waterston had been interested in the role of Marc. While later renowned for *The Killing Fields* (1984) and his tenure on *Law & Order* (1994-2010), at this time Waterston had a long list of highly acclaimed supporting roles behind him but hadn't quite broken through. Waterston eventually dropped out, busy with other commitments.

Anna too would prove difficult to secure. While Isabelle Adjani was Żuławski's first choice for the role, she would turn it down when first offered. Żuławski had been blown away by her performance in a recording of the play *Ondine* (Wybon 2009). In his director's commentary for *Possession*, Żuławski describes her talent in the French theatre, having had "this incredible sexual magic, even at fifteen" (Żuławski 2000). By the late 1970s, Adjani was well established, already having worked with Polanksi, Herzog, and Truffaut amongst others. According to Żuławski, Adjani had objected to playing the role of a mother. The search for Anna continued.

The casting process would turn again when Reyre and Żuławski saw Gillian Armstrong's *My Brilliant Career* at the 1979 Cannes Film Festival. Both producer and director were impressed by this quaint, turn-of-the-century Australian romance starring Judy Davis and Sam Neill, considering the pair as potential leads in *Possession* (Bird 2009a). While Davis and Neill undoubtedly gave fine performances, it is curious that Żuławski and Reyre saw in them the seeds of Anna and Marc. It is even more peculiar to think that Sybylla and Harry were very nearly plucked from the Australian countryside and dropped into Cold War Europe in something like *My Brilliant Career: Berlin Drift*.

Instincts were not off, however. For Żuławski, it was not just Neill's talent, but his humanity that impressed upon him in Armstrong's film (Bonitzer & Toubiana 1981: 44). Where Anna bursts in and out of *Possession*, Marc is almost always on screen. Żuławski needed someone that could be the connective tissue capable of holding the film together. Glimpses of Neill's capacity for volatility were already evident in Roger Donaldson's political thriller *Sleeping Dogs* (1977), and Armstrong's film had cemented Neill's caliber as a leading man. In *Possession*, Neill achieves an exceptional performance, fierce in both its intensity and sensitivity.

Satellite roles were largely populated by German talent. Margit Carstensen would play Anna's friend, Margie. Carstensen was well regarded in the German theatre, but also known for her numerous collaborations with Rainer Werner Fassbinder. Even in this relatively minor role, Carstensen exudes a charismatic sadism reminiscent of Petra von Kant. Anna's lover, Heinrich would be played by Heinz Bennent, also with a heritage in the German theatre. By this time, Bennent also had a long list of credits in German television, and had appeared in films by Ingmar Bergman, François Truffaut, and Volker Schlöndorff.

That Adjani did at last come to play Anna is another instance of faith or chance, depending on who is telling the story. After her initial rejection, Żuławski was busy recruiting his crew, including Bruno Nuytten who he wanted as cinematographer after seeing *The Brontë Sisters* (Téchiné 1979) (Bonitzer & Toubiana 1981: 46). According to Reyre, upon reading the script, Nuytten suggested that Adjani would be a great fit for the role, having already photographed her in André Téchiné's *Barocco* (1976) and *The Brontë Sisters* (Bird 2009a). Lamenting that Adjani had already rejected the role, Żuławski explained that he was at a loss for ideas. Żuławski claims he was unaware that Nuytten and Adjani were a couple, and so was unsure what to make of Nuytten's response: "Can you wait 24 hours?" (Wybon 2009). With Nuytten's intervention, Żuławski and Reyre would get their Anna. Schneidre envisions this less as a chance encounter, suggesting that Żuławski was likely well aware of Nuytten's connection to Adjani and that this was a calculated move (2017: 204). For reasons explained at the beginning of this chapter, however, Schneidre's account is necessarily unreliable. In any case, Adjani would agree to play Żuławski's ex-wife. Adjani's lover, Nuytten would photograph her. Żuławski would oversee everything. Another 'fundamentally vulgar structure', to use Heinrich's words, was forming.

PRODUCTION

...everything is pretty high pitched throughout this film. And so it was on set. – Sam Neill (personal communication, March 14, 2019)

There were obviously problems, psychological problems, a lot of things happened during this film. – Andrzej Żuławski (qtd. in Bonitzer & Toubiana 1981: 46)

Volkspolizei peer up at Possession's *crew from their post in the East.*

Possession's budget was set at $2.4 million USD and shooting commenced on July 7, 1980 on a twelve-week schedule (Bird 2009a). By all accounts, this was a trying affair, but how could it not be? Even if the shoot had run like clockwork, the physical and emotional pitch of such demanding performances alone would have made for an agitated atmosphere. Being a low budget film, time constraints were also a constant pressure. The apartment in which much of the shoot took place was tiny and within its cramped walls Żuławski was staging a deeply personal and painful Punch and Judy show. All of this would play out against the background of an active Cold War—armed VoPos watching the crew suspiciously from their posts mere meters away.

Neill has reflected on the remarkable atmosphere of Berlin at this time: "It was a largely empty city and strangely atmospheric. The ghosts of WW2, the Weimar Republic, of Nazism, and of the Prussian empire were everywhere. There were still bullet holes in the fabric of buildings" (personal communication, March 14, 2019). Beyond its metaphorical weight, the fraught nature of the city lends an eerie tone to the film.

Also contributing to *Possession*'s strange air is the collision of worlds it throws together. The production was a cultural hodgepodge: a Polish director shooting an English-language film in Germany, with leads that hailed from France and New Zealand. At this time, Neill had done very little work outside of Australia and New Zealand: "It was a weird time and a weird place. Everybody spoke English, but in a strange way that is reflected in the film's dialogue. I was really a man out of place" (S. Neill, personal communication, March 14, 2019). Conversely, many of the crew had experienced firsthand the communist regime of the Eastern bloc. Here they were now on the Western border looking back at it.

Unsurprisingly, tensions were high. Bruno Nuytten had to adjust to Żuławski's directorial style: absolute control. Żuławski describes himself as coming from a "poor man's cinema," in which the director has only as much film as is necessary, and so there is little room for trial and error. Instead, he knows exactly where he wants the camera having already seen and edited the film in his head (Wybon 2009). More habituated to Żuławski's temperament was Andrzej Jaroszewicz, the camera operator. Having worked on *The Devil*, *The Important Thing is to Love*, and *On the Silver Globe*, Jaroszewicz had already proven himself an invaluable asset in realising Żuławski's frenetic visual style. Żuławski had come to think of Jaroszewicz as "a second skin" who could work with him in symbiotic tandem (Bonitzer & Toubiana 1981: 47). By contrast, Żuławski asserts that while an incredibly gifted and intelligent cinematographer, Nuytten was unaccustomed to having so little creative input, finding himself somewhat relegated from the Polish faction of the crew (Bonitzer & Toubiana 1981: 46-7). Every decision would be debated.

Nuytten would handle the lighting. Jaroszewicz would follow Żuławski's camera direction to the millimeter.

While there was no room for trial, there was still room for error. In the climactic staircase sequence, when Anna introduces Marc to his double, the latter was supposed to have the same piercing green eyes as Anna's double, Helen. A clean-cut Neill walked up the stairs with coloured lenses in his sockets to create the effect, however, their lighter hue failed to photograph. Żuławski complains that Nuytten, so enamoured with Adjani, neglected to do the tests that would have pre-empted the issue: "He should have the eyes of the other woman, the very, very blue, clean, clear eyes of a monster... but they were brown in the film and I hated this D.O.P. ever after" (Żuławski 2000).

Żuławski has also described the tension borne of recreating the painful moments of his personal history. In a confused dynamic of art imitating life only to be turned into life imitating art, Żuławski explains the unsettling experience of watching actors recreate his marital breakdown while the present marital tensions between his lead and his Director of Photography bled back into his narrative. According to Żuławski (2000), Adjani treated Nuytten "with the upmost cruelty" throughout the shoot. In effect, Anna's malice—particularly in Heinrich's home video when she torments a ballet student—was even more acute than the director had originally envisioned. At the same time, Żuławski was confronted by the memories of his divorce, like not-so-distant ghosts revitalised.

If Adjani behaved cruelly—and I only have Żuławski's side of this story—her cruelty was surely no match for that shown towards her by Żuławski, himself. To this, there are conflicting accounts. The director has admitted to treating Adjani badly in order to extract the performance he desired, however, the level of personal complicity he perceives in her unhappy relationship to *Possession* seems to dissipate over time. While I will return to this thread a little later when I unpack Żuławski's approach to directing performance in more depth, for now it is worth acknowledging one disturbing example openly recounted by the director as it gives insight into the atmosphere on set.

Early in the shoot, when one of Helen's scenes were due to be filmed, Żuławski explains that Adjani objected to wearing the artificial lenses that turned her eyes green. According to Żuławski, he arrived on set to find her very upset, her face swollen and red. After some conversation, Żuławski discerned that the head of makeup, Roland

Abreau, had told Adjani that the green eyes made her look ugly. Furious at her refusal to transform into character, Żuławski resorted to threatening Adjani with violence. As Żuławski recounts the story in a 2009 interview, he "pushed her behind a door, pressed it against her and said, 'Isabelle, if you don't get downstairs in 10 minutes, ready to shoot like you should, I'll crush you with this door. And if you come downstairs without those eyes, I will kill you'" (qtd. in Wybon 2009). The director then casually relates that Adjani complied, the scene was shot, and there was no further incident between them.

At other times, threats to the cast and crew were made by a generally cavalier approach to low-budget filmmaking. One need only watch *Possession* to get a sense of a kind of reckless abandon in the pursuit of capturing its images. When Marc chases Anna from the apartment into the street, a tow truck swerves, narrowly missing the cast before spilling car wrecks across the cobblestones, one skidding to rest dangerously close to the camera. Over the course of the film, we will see Marc leap from a moving taxi, spectacularly crash a motorcycle, and finally throw himself from the spiral stairwell of the Joseph-Hadyn Palais. According to Żuławski (2000), the stunts are as insane as they appear: "As we were short of money, we used Yugoslav stunt people...and they were like 15 crazy guys, totally drunk from morning to night who were saying 'listen, Andrzej, if you want - I jump from this building and BANG my head 15 floors!...It will be beautiful!' I said 'no please don't, there is no use to do it!'" One intoxicated and overzealous stunt double, Żuławski recalls, insisted on landing every stunt headfirst, causing numerous injuries.

Eagerness of the crew aside, there's no question that Żuławski also pursued his vision at the expense of its constituent's safety. Neill recalls the foolhardy demands of his director when shooting the scene in which Marc escapes authorities on a speeding motorcycle. "I had never ridden a motorbike before and had just a day or two to learn, and ended up driving a 1000cc Honda at speed around Berlin, seemingly centimetres from a speeding vehicle carrying the camera crew. This was positively dangerous" (S. Neill, personal communication, March 14, 2019). Marc's bike will eventually skid and crash where Neill's stunt double is dragged by gravity across the coarse pavement for a least a meter before being thrown and spun in the air to land on his shoulder, rolling further across the ground. This image feels raw because it is. There is no buffer or digital manipulation — we are simply witnessing a man collide with a hard surface at speed.

Żuławski (2000) recounts this incredibly risky effect as being the work of a talented Austrian stunt performer. Beyond the obvious dangers of landing on concrete, the rider only had a range of approximately four metres in which to complete the manoeuvre because the industrial lot in which he crashes borders the Spree river. Had the stunt been miscalculated, the performer would have been thrown into East German waters and subsequently arrested.

Neill's stunt double throws himself from a motorcycle at high speed.

SCRIPT ADJUSTMENTS

His work apparently over, Tuten was surprised to receive a call from Żuławski during the shoot explaining that a character needed to be written out of the script (Iatrou & Morgan 2019). The character was Abe, Anna's former husband. This seemed a radical alteration so late in the game, Abe having been cast (Bernhard Wicki) and on-set ready to perform. "I thought he was out of his mind," Tuten recalls at hearing Żuławski's plan (qtd. in Iatrou & Morgan 2019). Regardless, the writer flew from Paris to Berlin and so began a process of cutting this narrative thread and fusing what remained back together again.

Żuławski has given varied accounts of why Abe needed to be expunged. In one instance, the director explains that it was in the process of shooting that he realised he had made a casting error in that Wicki was not embodying Abe the way he had envisioned. Moreover, Żuławski came to feel Abe's character was detracting from the clarity of the film (Bird 2009a). In another instance, the director charges Wicki with being perpetually drunk and unable to recall his lines, an unacceptable burden upon an already tight shooting schedule (Żuławski 2000). In any case, the removal of Abe marks a significant difference between shooting script and completed film, and this lacuna is worth consideration.

Abe was to appear at three intervals during the film: at the beginning, middle, and end. In the film's first scene (of which no trace remains), Abe is described as a "huge, old man…looking a bit drunk and unkempt." Abe runs into Marc on a crowded street, and seeing that Marc is tormented over Anna, he tells him a parable about Tolstoy's drafting of *Anna Karenina*. Tolstoy, he claims, set out to "write a novel against women because he despised his own wife." Originally titled *The Devil*, Abe explains that the novel's title was amended when its author discovered that in spite of his intentions, during the writing process the heroine was elevated while the male characters became petty and debased.

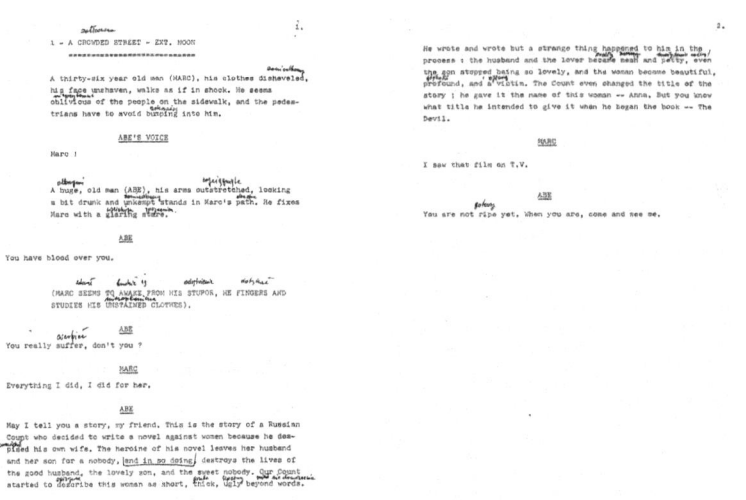

The opening scene - cut from Possession *during shooting. Courtesy of Oliane Productions.*

The film as we know it, begins with the scene that follows this one in the screenplay: Marc's return to the family apartment on Bernauerstraße. While *Possession* is still very much told from Marc's point of view—he is in almost every scene—had this exchange between Marc and Abe remained, the film would have made its male perspective even more totalising.

This shaping of our understanding of Anna is continued in another scene that was to precede Marc's meeting with Zimmerman at the detective agency (it is Abe's suggestion that Marc employ a detective to trace Anna). As in the first scene, Abe is figured like a wise old guide who offers Marc counsel through misogynist rumination. Notably, Abe's dialogue provides a frame through which to interpret Anna's behaviour. Without these intervals, Anna is a mystery to us; we, like Marc strain to understand Anna the enigma.

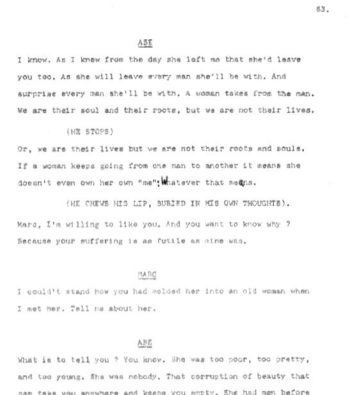

An excerpt from a cut scene. Abe counsels Marc about Anna. Courtesy of Oliane Productions.

In this scene, we are also introduced to Sara (likely a reference to Sarah, wife of Abraham in the Old Testament), Abe's pretty, and much younger romantic interest. Abe describes their coupling in biblical terms: "The old testament, my dear. I am the shepherd near the well, watering my dromaderies [sic]. She walks by, a clay vase on her shoulder... I am seducing her, of course. Sweet as a fig..." Having served the men some tea, Sara leaves the room. While Abe looks on longingly, and later mocks Marc for not having noticed her beauty, in the screen direction we are told: "Marc can see that one of her shoulders is slightly deformed and that one foot is slightly twisted inward." It is a curious detail. Is Marc's perspective to be trusted? Are we to take this as indication that he perceives women as monstrous?

Adding to the biblical resonance, this scene also introduces the idea of apocalypse. Abe pushes Marc up some stairs to a platform overlooking the city and delivers a prophetic monologue:

> There are no wives anymore, no pairs, no couples. There is a pattern, a mean god, a black star, a black hole moving close in the sky and sucking us in, this city, this whole world doomed; a surrendering of the lights I'm witnessing here, the last one to remember. Remember. Remember what?

In the screenplay, Abe then flies into a rage and begins physically assaulting Marc, the scene ending shortly after when Abe experiences heart trouble for which he must take medication. Of course, in the finished film, the apocalyptic ending comes without warning.

Finally, Abe was due to appear at the film's climax. According to the screenplay, it is the sight of Marc's doppelgänger on the spiral staircase that causes Abe to go into cardiac arrest. This time he refuses medical attention at the hands of Sara. It is interesting to note that where Abe has been entirely erased, a trace of Sara does remain in this climactic scene. It is Sara, her leg in a cast, who aids the creature's escape through the open window in the roof. In the film as we know it, she is a stranger to us, her presence at the top of the stairway incidental and enigmatic.

There is some irony in the removal of Abe, given the parable about Tolstoy that was to open the film. Just as the Russian Count's depiction of his wife was unconsciously tempered during the creative process, Żuławski's removal of Abe pares back the film's anger towards women. There are other instances too where cuts to the script have had this effect, most notably the removal of a brief scene in which a slightly drunk and self-assured Marc enters "a respectable looking bar" only to discover it populated entirely by women. "Swollen with hatred" the screenplay tells us, Marc approaches the female bartender who voices the only lines of dialogue in the scene: "This is a lesbian bar, Sir. Are you a lesbian?" Had this scene been included, I have to assume it would have played as a comic moment at Marc's expense.

The most openly misogynistic moment in the film that remains (aside from Marc's physical and verbal abuse of Anna) is his dialogue in the scene between himself and Helen when he explains he is "at war against women." This scene too plays to comic effect, however; Helen astutely disarms his arrogance brushing aside his observations as "pathetic." While I will explore this moment in more detail in the next chapter, here I will note that this exchange has always felt to me to an oddity that the effacement of Abe helps to clarify. Though these words were always intended for Marc, with the added context of Abe as a guiding figure, they are shaded with an added resonance. To me, Marc appears to be affecting a persona, as though he were trying out Abe's brand of sexist philosophical musings like an ill-fitting costume that Helen quickly dismisses.

While Żuławski has suggested that Abe was an obfuscatory element in the narrative that proved unnecessary, in some ways it seems his presence clarifies an interpretation of events—Anna's behaviour is manipulative and callous because she does not know herself, and it is women's nature; the world is foreordained to ruin, and so on. However, like the trite explanation offered by the psychiatrist at the end of Hitchcock's *Psycho* (1960), this framing feels like an imposition, its reading unsatisfactory. Tuten has reflected that he feels the film is ultimately better for having cut this character, suggesting that Żuławski had likely realised that while Abe holds significance in an autobiographic sense (he too is inspired by someone in Żuławski's past), this character burdened the story (Bird 2009a).

THE MONSTER

Seeking a friend's opinion on *Possession*'s script, Żuławski recounts being advised that the monster never be shown (Thrower & Bird 2003: 70). This advice was evidently dismissed; Żuławski found such a suggestion to be antithetical to the medium of cinema, the virtue of which is *to show*. Marie-Laure Reyre recounted in a 1982 interview, "It was a big decision to show or not to show…or maybe, just show a little as in *Rosemary's Baby*, when you never fully saw that was happening, but you certainly felt it" (qtd. in Crawley 1982: 17). This latter understanding seems to have been Tuten's, who was shocked to discover during shooting that Żuławski intended to feature the monster. In Tuten's interpretation of the screenplay, the monster is an ambiguous presence glimpsed in a flicker of light or obscured by the *mise en scène* (Bird 2009a).

It's not entirely surprising that even the film's co-writer was expecting the creature to be an enigma. Originally, Żuławski had envisioned the monster as an unstable entity—Anna would recount her memory of how it came into being, not only to Marc, as we see in her recollection of the subway sequence, but to other characters as well. With each explanation, Anna's account would vary, casting more doubt onto its veracity. In one of the versions that Żuławski explains was abandoned during shooting, Anna's miscarriage of the monster is less an involuntary evacuation than a willful act of creation. Recounting her experience in the U-Bahn tunnel, Anna sees an eye in some sand on the subway floor. Kneading the sand with the slimy contents of her shopping that she has smashed against the wall, Anna creates something like the clay from which the golem is molded in Jewish folklore[1] (Bonitzer & Toubiana 1981: 43).

Once the decision was made to show rather than tell, the search for someone to realise Żuławski's monster began. Reyre and Żuławski began scouting for special effects talent in France, England, and Germany (Crawley 1982: 17). Żuławski recalls the challenge: "It was difficult because I found myself in front of technicians, to whom it was especially necessary to explain that it should not look like anything. But to look like nothing is to look like what?" (qtd. in Bonitzer & Toubiana 1981: 43). The opening of Ridley Scott's *Alien* (1979) prompted director and producer to approach H.R. Giger. Already immersed in work on multiple films, Giger recommended Carlo Rambaldi. With an extensive slate of effects experience in Italian cinema, by the mid-1970s Rambaldi was working on Hollywood blockbusters including *King Kong* (Guillermin 1976), *Close Encounters of the Third Kind* (Spielberg 1977), and *Alien*. Reyre and Żuławski met with Rambaldi who was at the time creating effects for Oliver Stone's *The Hand* (1981). Designs and miniatures were circulated as Rambaldi began working on *Possession*'s monster; however, the product he arrived with on-set would set in stark reality the gap between concept and delivery.

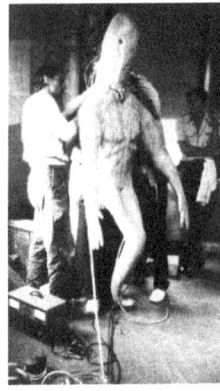
The monster on set. Courtesy of Oliane Productions.

Marie-Laure Reyre, who was waiting for Rambaldi at the airport along with Executive Producer, Jean-José Richer, recalls the situation at Tegel airport. Rambaldi was stopped by West Berlin officers curious as to the contents of the five large coffin-like crates he was importing. Producing a letter from the Senate of Berlin proved unsatisfactory, so one can only imagine what the officers thought when Rambaldi reluctantly opened one of the boxes, revealing a mass of unruly tentacles. Startled, the officers promptly retreated (Crawley 1982: 17; Bird 2009a).

When *E.T.* (1982) wrapped, Rambaldi remembers Spielberg thanking him for his efficiency (Martin 1985: 45). On *Possession*, the effects artist would receive no such praise. According to Żuławski, Rambaldi arrived on set having completely miscalculated the urgency with which the completed creature was required for shooting. Accustomed to the lumbering pace and precision of big-budget American productions, Rambaldi was anticipating extensive camera tests, in response to which his creation would be painted and refined. When Rambaldi's monster was unveiled on set, Żuławski was unimpressed. Recalling his first impression, the director said: "He's made a huge contraption, a huge guy, a pink guy, like three meters high, resembling a condom...we couldn't shoot with that" (Żuławski 2000). No doubt embarrassed, Rambaldi explained that Reyre had advised that the creature was a sexual symbol. Żuławski, incredulous, responded: "This is not a symbol, it's a penis! You made the thing. It's just as if I filmed you without your underwear" (qtd. in Wybon 2009). Informed that the monster was to be shot the following morning, the effects artist turned pale. Rambaldi would soon regain his resolve, however, working through the night with two assistants in a hotel room to transform this mass of pink latex into the glistening, pulsating monstrosity we first glimpse in the Kreuzberg apartment bathroom (Żuławski 2000).

For Żuławski, the monster remained a painful memory. Rambaldi, unprepared, was not able to realise the creature in the way Żuławski wanted (Żuławski 2000). Reyre, who was quite pleased with the creature, remembers things differently. When asked in a 1982 interview how Żuławski reacted to seeing Rambaldi's creation, Reyre states that there was no confrontation; having visited Rambaldi in the States six times to see the design in progress, he knew what to expect. The producer admits, however, that the tight budget made for time constraints and Rambaldi's scenes would push them over schedule (Crawley 1982: 18).

With more time, with more money, in a cinema that was not a poor man's cinema, perhaps the monster would have complex automated mechanics to facilitate its movement. But time and money were two things *Possession* had little of. A blockbuster like *E.T.* could afford its creature a complex design—the alien had 85 points of movement, "just like a human being," Ramaldi recalls with pride (qtd. in Martin 1985: 45). At most, *Possession*'s monster had four or five (Martin 1985: 46). Making it move would require a wealth of effort from an already stretched crew. Describing the scene in which Zimmerman sees the creature writhing in Anna's bed as "like an early animation film from the 1900s," Żuławski (2000) remembers having his assistant lay underneath the creature manipulating its arms and legs through a hole in the mattress. At the same time, with much perspiration and colourful language, several crew members pulled attachments to move its limbs and head.

The infamous sex scene between Anna and the monster (now half man, half tentacles) was likewise rudimentary in its technical realisation. "We had three assistants glued to the mattress," Żuławski (2000) laughs. "As we never had the monster, we had to deal with a very primitive contraption, things to make it move". Reyre recalls Neill's stand-in rigged up to Rambaldi's tentacled creation, "it was something quite heavy, he was in a very uncomfortable situation" (qtd. in Crawley 1982: 18). Adjani, exposed and having to wholeheartedly simulate passion under such circumstances no doubt also felt this to be a demanding day. "She was very brave because she was like the object," Żuławski remembers. "We started to shoot at six in the evening and she had her clothes on at, I think, like four in the morning" (Żuławski 2000). This scene, however, hardly marked the limits of Adjani's discomfort.

Bad blood, trance states, and going beyond one's limits

> I owe it to the mystique of Andrzej Żuławski to have revealed to me things I wish I had never discovered. *Possession* was an unfeasible film, and what I did in that film was just as unfeasible. However, I did it and what happened on this film cost me so much… Despite all the awards, all the honors that have gone to me, never again a trauma like that, a nightmare! – Isabelle Adjani (qtd. in Klifa & Lavoignat 2002: 75)

Anna's miscarriage in the U-Bahn tunnel, described at the opening of this book, is as notorious as it is extraordinary. How did Adjani get into the headspace that allowed her to move and emote with such abandon? And what direction did Żuławski give her that translated into this otherworldly expression? To the former question—not without lasting suffering. To the latter question—apparently very little. According to Adjani, Żuławski's direction in this scene consisted of three words: "Fuck the air" (Bird 2009b). The director admits this was a rare moment in which he was at a loss for words. "Usually you explain, you talk. How can you explain something which you cannot explain yourself?" (Żuławski qtd. in Bird 2009a).

The shoot would take place in the early morning hours in one of the pedestrian tunnels at the Platz der Luftbrücke U-Bahn station. In the bitter cold, Adjani would give everything she had, and perhaps more, to create cinema's most arresting portrayal of hysteria. Screaming and laughter, convulsions and hyperventilation, Adjani appears to be in the throes of a violent exorcism. At one point, her head collides with the tiled wall but her thrashing persists unabated; if you listen carefully you can hear it—a sickening thud.

Though deeply unsettling to watch, there is something transcendental about this scene. Żuławski, who is often eager to claim credit for the achievements of his cast and crew, in this instance defers. Speaking of Adjani's performance in this scene, Żuławski said: "For me, it's a great performance. I'm happy to say it because I was more a witness than a director…for me, there it's as if it weren't my film. It's a great moment where an actress gives something you rarely see" (qtd. in Wybon 2009). For her co-star, this performance marked a moment of revelation. Though not present for this part of the shoot, Neill recalls seeing the footage for the first time: "This was when I realised we were doing something at a completely different level. She was incandescent" (personal communication, March 14, 2019).

Isabelle Adjani in Possession's *infamous subway scene.*

Adjani's performance throughout *Possession* is phenomenal and would be awarded as such with both the Cannes prize for Best Actress as well as a César. Neill expresses the utmost admiration of her talent: "I don't think I've ever worked with anyone who was so vividly present in each mad moment. She was extraordinary" (personal communication, March 14, 2019). Indeed, Adjani conveys limit states of emotional expression that surpass anything I have personally seen in cinema before or since. At times her body conveys psychic distress with such gravity that she seems to be desperate to escape her own skin. One wonders, however, what embodying such a performance and channelling such madness costs its author. According to Adjani: too high a price.

It is no secret that Adjani was deeply affected by her experience shooting *Possession*, once describing the film with disdain as a work of "emotional pornography" (Adjani qtd. in Borkowski 1981: 7). She has a point. Performances in *Possession*, and in many of Żuławski's films are characterized by physical and emotional extremes. Bodies on screen are moved in something like religious ecstasy, Żuławski eliciting performances that are horrifyingly raw, but always mesmerising. "It's like my skin is ripped off and you can see inside," Adjani continues. "It swarms in my head and comes out bubbling" (qtd. in Borkowski 1981: 7). This is not pornography in the sense of excess for the sake of spectator pleasure, but perhaps better understood in the sense of Linda Williams's notion of a pornographic "frenzy of the visible," that is, the revelatory quality of bearing witness to what the perception of bodies moved can tell us (1989: 36). Witnessing these actors unravel emotionally in all their twisting, contorting and shuddering, one gets the feeling of being given access to something forbidden. Adjani in particular seems very often on the brink of a real breakdown, so unhinged is her expression and physicality.

That Żuławski gets such unbridled performances from his cast, not only in *Possession*, but across all his films, is a significant part of what makes his work so striking. How he garners these performances, however, is something that Adjani's difficult experience on-set has since called into question. In an interview at the 1981 Cannes film festival when *Possession* premiered, Adjani describes the way Żuławski would manipulate his cast, observing for their weak points in order to know how to make them crack (Adjani 1981). In a separate interview at the same festival, Żuławski admits:

> It was a very hard shoot for [Adjani], very difficult for many reasons…at the end of the second day there was a huge psychodrama between us because she was a frozen character, afraid to show herself, afraid of herself, not knowing if she has the right to draw from her life. I don't pretend to have the therapeutic keys at all, but I knew what I needed, and so I cruelly played somewhere, I pressed where I had to press, that's all, regardless of what it might do to her as good or bad, but it's part of this job which is a very cruel job. (qtd. in Bonitzer & Toubiana 1981: 46)

Later, however, Żuławski would be dismissive of Adjani's accusations. In his director's commentary, recorded in 2000, he argues that it was Adjani's refusal to watch the footage captured during the shoot that left her unprepared for how she appeared. In this same commentary, Żuławski also claims that after finally seeing *Possession*, Adjani attempted suicide by superficially cutting her wrists, though likewise dismisses this as the theatrical and disingenuous behaviour of a "diva." I haven't been able to confirm this claim as any more than rumour, though it is an anecdote Żuławski has recounted elsewhere (Skoczen 2000; Thrower & Bird 2003: 62).

What is clear, is that Adjani felt manipulated by Żuławski, at one point describing him as a magician (Bird 2003b: 367). While this may sound like an exaggeration, perhaps we should not be so quick to dismiss it. Notoriously reluctant to discuss his methods in directing performances, Żuławski did open up somewhat in a 1997 interview:

> I went several times to Haiti, I was very interested in the experiments of [Jerzy] Grotowski, a very famous, avant-garde Polish director, working there for thirty years. The trance phenomenon. What is it? Nobody knows. Does it exist? Yes, I can put you into a trance, in about twenty minutes, and you won't know what you'll be doing. So it's profoundly human, it's in you, but if you refuse that basic darkness, psychological darkness, in which you can walk over fire or pierce yourself with a sword and nothing happens to you, if you don't admit it, you don't understand anything about acting, about the performing arts, at all. I like pushing actors to the border of this sometimes...So in order to open my actors, I have an assistant I love, who organizes this with me, and we devise little programs, 3,4,5 days, so they go into deep trance. We never talk about it, they always ask 'What happened', we say 'Nothing.' (qtd. in Thrower & Bird 2003: 66)

There are two threads I want to pull here. The first is Żuławski's reference to Grotowski, the theatre revolutionary whom he cites as an influence; the second is the problematic way in which Żuławski implies he has incorporated this influence.

Grotowski has a long and rich history of theoretical approaches and practical experiments in performance, and while there isn't scope to explore these in detail, it is worth noting that he was interested in developing exercises via which performers might access unconscious memories (Laster 2016: 22) and liberate the body from conditioning that blocks the creative process (Laster 2016: 27). These techniques are deeply introspective, requiring a total and unguarded offering of oneself. According to Grotowski, a performer must treat their role "as if it were a surgeon's scalpel, to dissect himself" (Grotowski 2002: 37).

Beyond one's limits.

When Grotowski describes his methodology in a 1967 interview, we get a better sense of his aesthetic kinship with Żuławski:

> When I say 'go beyond yourself' I am asking for an insupportable effort. One is obliged not to stop despite fatigue and to do things that we know well we cannot do. That means one is also obliged to be courageous. What does this lead to? There are certain points of fatigue which break control of the mind, a control that blocks us. When we find the courage to do things that are impossible, we make the discovery that our body does not block us. We do the impossible and the division within us between conception and the body's ability disappears. This attitude, this determination, is a training for how to go beyond our limits. These are not the limits of our nature, but those of our discomfort. (Grotowski 2002: 248-9)

Żuławski's approach to directing takes up Grotowski's cues, attempting to "unblock" actors from societal conditioning, and both directors have described acting in spiritual terms.[2] It is true Grotowski theorised about trance states in developing his methodologies of performance. Crucially, however, trance states, for Grotowski are not unconscious, but are characterised rather by an elevated awareness. Only in an "unhealthy trance" is awareness diminished (Slowiak & Cuesta 2018: 62).

While Żuławski has claimed that Adjani was always aware of what she was doing, employing the exercises in a very conscious way (Thrower & Bird 2003: 66), his posturing about trance states in the quote above raises a question of consent. Is it possible that Żuławski used Grotowski's methods in bad faith? There is a significant difference between the admittedly painful act of revealing one's most private and intimate self (what Grotowski [2002: 35] refers to as "self-penetration") and the same self-exposure when unwitting. In a 1998 interview, Żuławski explained that, as opposed to Grotowski, who "doesn't provide a safety net for actors," he would try to incorporate a buffer for performers:

> ...I'm asking these actors and actresses to do things which may even seem revolting to some, these scenes of trances... But they risk nothing, after fifteen minutes they laugh and they go, they go and play at the Comédie-Française or do idiotic plays, it doesn't affect them, it doesn't hurt. (qtd. in Bird 2012)

What are we to make of these conflicting accounts? Even if the truth is somewhere in the middle between these two extremes, it is still unsettling. While Adjani's performance in *Possession* is exceptional, it is indeed indicative of a performer who has pushed beyond her limits.

At times, Neill would also be pressured out of his comfort zone by the demands of his director. While Adjani's performance often takes centre stage in discussions of this film—and it is incredible—we should not overlook Neill's remarkable contribution. His too is a role which requires physical and emotional extremes, not least in the scene where Marc confines himself to a hotel room and undergoes a mental breakdown. Pallid like a corpse, his body shivers and sweats, clenches and rocks—his entire physique recruited into an expression of mental anguish. Describing his experience playing Marc, Neill has said:

> It certainly was emotionally draining and, what's more, physically exhausting. It was necessary to follow Żuławski into this kind of frenzied excess. He demanded nothing less. I remember at the end of each day retreating to my hotel, running a bath and lying there listening to Genesis thinking: 'What is this crazy shit I've got myself into?' And then the next day having to get up and do it all again. But then everybody, cast and crew, were stretched beyond the limits of what they imagined were possible. And

I sort of feel that it was worth it. (personal communication, March 14, 2019)

While Neill's experience of working with Żuławski was more positive than Adjani's, he too was subject to difficult moments fuelled by the director's uncompromising vision. If, as Żuławski has claimed, Adjani was in a trance state and therefore did not feel her head colliding with the subway wall (Żuławski 2000; Thrower & Bird 2003: 66), Neill was not buffered by such exercises. Vividly, he recalls the pain of being wrestled to the ground by several men, some larger than himself, in the Café Einstein scene. Most challenging, however, was the scene in which Marc strikes Anna in the face during an argument. Neill objected to this direction, insisting that such things were simulated in cinema, however, both Żuławski and Adjani insisted that the slap be authentic.

> We had three takes. Three times I had to hit Isabelle Adjani. This was the first and last time I have ever raised a hand to anyone, let alone a woman. I was deeply distressed by this and found a staircase/fire escape place outside the apartment and found myself in tears alone on the stairs. I suspect if Żuławski had found me there he would have regarded my distress as a bit feeble. And this was the thing about Żuławski – he could be a bully and arrogant; but a genius for all that. And it was all in the name, I guess, of achieving excellence. Now while I always want to do my best for whatever director I am working for, I doubt I would allow myself to be bullied into that again. (S. Neill, personal communication, March 14, 2019)

The impact of *Possession*, like any work of art, can exist independent of a knowledge of its machinery. Like the strings Żuławski's crew pulled to make the creature move, the creative mechanism is designed to be invisible. But what are we to do with the knowledge attained by gazing behind the curtain? In many ways, I think this knowledge fosters our appreciation of *Possession*; in other ways, it cannot help but pollute it. My goal is here is neither to demonise nor idolise Żuławski, rather I have tried to present varied perspectives of what, by all accounts, was an arduous shoot.

It would be irresponsible of me to assume a definitive understanding of the nature of *Possession*'s production. I cannot know for certain that Adjani was in a trance state when she entered the U-Bahn tunnel, nor the extent to which she was consciously willing her performance. I cannot know how many other stories from that summer in Berlin remain untold, just as I cannot know with certitude just how exaggerated or downplayed some of the stories that have been told are. While I of course hold reservations about the methods Żuławski employed to attain the performances and images therein, the fact is that *Possession* remains an extraordinary achievement. The next chapter offers an analysis of this astonishing film.

FOOTNOTES

1. Evidence suggesting at least some of this sequence was shot surfaced in the US cut of *Possession*, which is covered in Chapter 4.
2. Żuławski's conviction that acting is spiritual is likely inherited from Grotowski's conceptualisation of performance. In a 1964 interview by Eugenio Barba entitled "The Theatre's New Testament," Grotowski outlines his concept of a "holy actor." The holy actor is not holy in a religious sense, but "rather a metaphor defining a person who, through his art, climbs upon the stake and performs and act of self-sacrifice" (Grotowski 2002: 43). Żuławski has evoked similar terms, stating: "it's impossible to forget that acting is religious, basically. The first actor is the shaman acting in front of his flock...We act because we are religious beasts" (qtd. in Thrower & Bird 2003: 66).

Chapter 3: Up the Spiral Staircase

> ...a staircase comes from basement to heaven. This movement...it's the *l'échelle de Jacob* in the Bible...I think that everything I do is to show always this tunnel, this murky part, this muddling, this struggling, and the light at the end which you can, or hopefully can attain. – Andrzej Żuławski (2000)

The spiral staircase is a recurring motif in Żuławski's films—characters ascend them, jump from them, are mistaken and murdered on them, give birth, and die on them. More than a nod towards Wajda's *A Generation*, for Żuławski the winding stairway informs a broader aesthetic patterning. Eric Veaux, who translated several of Żuławski's novels from Polish to French observed that his written works "had a sort of spiral-shaped literary construction. You start with a character or a theme, you go up and around in a circle and arrive back where you were before, but one level higher" (E. Veaux qtd. in Guigou 2014). As convoluted and disorienting as *Possession* seems, with this patterning in mind we can endeavor to trace the film's repetitions and digressions towards a better understanding. With its doppelgängers and echoed scenes, Żuławski's formal logic in *Possession* keeps leading us somewhere that is the same but different; via this complex but elegant symmetry that promotes movement, one progresses but appears to be perpetually returning. In this chapter then, I'd like to think about *Possession*'s structure like the staircase at its heart, tracking round and round, its characters striving to break with the fleshy, impure material world and all its suffering, moving instead towards the transcendental. But we must watch the couple finish their descent into hell before they can climb out of it.

1. Material

'Coming home from the wars, so to speak'

The first images we see in *Possession* are of the Berlin Wall. A bleak overcast sky hangs over Eastern Bloc tenements, the blockade stretching into the distance. An anonymous cross adorned with barbed wire and flowers serves as the grim marker of a failed attempt at escape. The ominous strings of Andrzej Korzyński's score shiver into existence, offset by the incongruously playful chime of a synth xylophone. Behind this, a drum pulses like an elevated heartbeat before a high-pitched flute screeches unnervingly. Taking Marc's perspective from the rear of a cab, our eyes trace the dilapidated house fronts along Bernauerstraße, once the scene of dramatic escapes as Easterners jumped to the West from apartment windows that have since been evacuated and bricked up. A simple line of graffiti across the brickwork protests 'Die Mauer muß weg!' (*The Wall must go!*).

It is a foreboding opening, amplified because this is not a set; for all the flourishes of surreal madness to come, Żuławski grounds us very much in the perilous real. It is, of course, entirely fitting that Żuławski chose to shoot his horrific testament to division and duality in Berlin. Marc is *en route* home to the apartment he shares with his estranged wife, Anna, and their young son, Bob, after a prolonged period of work in the East. To the West, and his family he returns, only to find that the stable foundations he left behind have eroded in his absence. What better backdrop for a violent separation than against what Norman Gelb would refer to as "that gruesome monument to human discord" (1986: 7)?

These opening moments are but the first of several instances in the film in which we will see the Wall as it stood in 1980. Several times we follow Marc's gaze out the apartment window at its grim concrete blocks and barbed wire fortifications. More than once, curious guards on its Eastern frontier peer up through binoculars, no doubt suspicious of the camera trained on them. The balcony of Anna's secret apartment in Kreuzberg hugs the Wall even closer; the infamous "death strip" mere meters away. Rows of tank traps—great lopsided crosses bound in barbed wire—are also visible. Producer, Marie Laure-Reyre recalls the crew's protections under the Senate of Berlin (Bird 2009a), but even so, we are looking into an historical present fraught with lethal tension.

Żuławski describes his decision to open the film with the Wall, "…to have this entrenched psychology of people surrounded by evil, and finally evil worms up into their universe" (qtd. in Bird 2009a). Both a literal and symbolic imposition, the Wall is a peripheral character in the film, always looming—the preeminent and impassive signifier of alienation through which Żuławski might literalise the emotional turmoil of his divorce. This 156 kilometres of concrete and steel that divides two Germanys, an attempt to establish a communist utopia, comes at the expense of its occupants, now imprisoned. This couple, the family unit, is another kind of attempt at establishing happiness, now on the verge of being stripped apart. *Die Mauer muβ weg!* But not before the human element is torn down and reassembled.

Anna and Marc divided in the frame.

The divided city frames a divided family. Our first look inside Marc and Anna's apartment partitions the couple as we simultaneously glimpse Anna busy in the kitchen, while Marc supervises their son's bath time from the entry to the adjacent bathroom. Żuławski often separates the couple within the same frame either in barriers within the *mise en scène*, or by isolating them in different planes of a shot's depth of field. This stylisation is at its most explicit when Marc and Anna meet at the Café Einstein to discuss arrangements. Before mirrored panels set at 90 degrees, the couple sit at rigid odds reflecting each other's posture, the emotional disjunct again absorbed by the *mise en scène*.

But if the couple is divided in domestic space, they are also thrust uncomfortably together. The apartment, and we will spend much of the film within its walls, becomes increasingly claustrophobic as tensions between the couple rise. "Excuse me," Anna will say, and then shout, pushing past the husband who crowds her in a kitchen that suddenly feels too small for the both of them. Emotionally distant and physically contained, Anna and Marc repel and collide like unstable atoms.

Domestic Horrors

Possession presents the ordinary, but it is the ordinary denaturalized. The streets are deathly quiet, a ghost of Berlin. Interiors are likewise nudged off-kilter, banal domestic settings filtered through an oppressively blue colour palette. We feel this in the family apartment in particular—carpet, walls, bathroom tiles, bed linen and lamps are all blue. Combined with wide-angle lenses that distort space and render everything significant, it is a vision of the everyday made strange. Dominique Schneidre describes the effect achieved, the camera "A kind of fly eye that sees everywhere, from floor to ceiling" (2017: 206). The lighting is cold, the tone clinical; Żuławski dissects his failing marriage like a surgeon.

In this way, the horror of *Possession* is first and foremost domestic—the home, relationships, family, divorce. Żuławski (2000) conceived of the domestic sphere as brimming with a latent violence, inevitable and inexorable, the accursed share of modernity: "People are locked in apartments...if you don't make war today, where's your rank? Where's the rank for your violence? For your impulses? It's a domestic rank, it's shrunk to something between a man and a woman, so: apartments, beds, bedrooms." Shared spaces become an emotional and physical battleground, their occupants bristling with tension that inevitably erupts.

Much of the pressure comes from an inability for the pair to communicate. For the first half of the film, the couple's arguments follow a pattern of antagonism and deterioration in which violence fills the void opened by a failure in understanding. Marc and Anna push, pull, and slap at each other as though grievances must be exorcised physically in the absence of coherent terms with which to make oneself or the other understood. Although pitched at emotional and physical extremes, at the core of Marc and Anna's arguments are the relatively ordinary albeit unpleasant disputes between estranged partners locked in a battle for ascendancy. The practicalities of financial support, living arrangements, and parental visitation rights are interspersed with the emotional fallout; Marc's insatiable thirst for the details of Anna's affair with which to wound and re-wound his ego bespeaks a level of masochism, and fuels barbed reproaches. Anna oscillates between wearily accepting Marc's labels and dishing back an acerbic serve of her own vitriol.

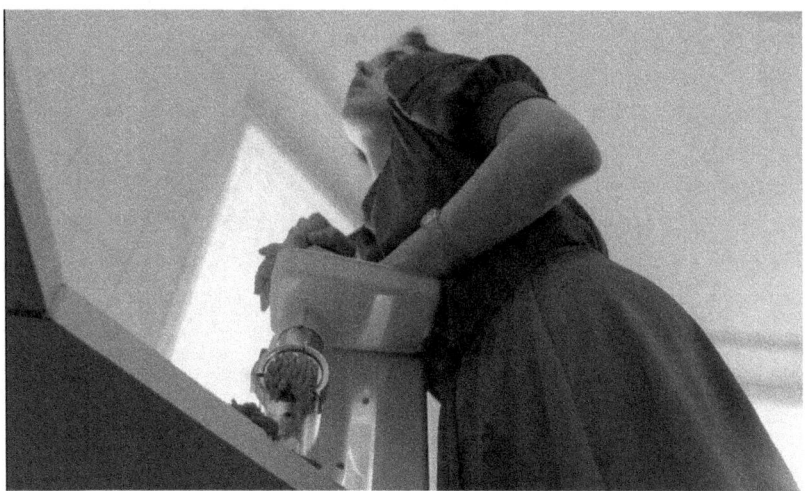

The everyday becomes horror in Possession.

During one argument, violence is turned against the self when the pressure to communicate becomes overwhelming. As Marc relentlessly bullies and then begs his wife for an explanation for her behaviour, Anna busies herself with kitchen chores seemingly incapable of more than nodding or shaking her head in response. Eventually, having exhausted himself, Marc turns away cradling his head in his hands, his barrage of questions dissipating into a desperate plea: "Help me." Anna stares vacantly ahead, raising an electric carving knife to her throat, her former silence broken with a succession of primal screams.

Horror erupts from the ordinary, with household items recruited to weaponry for use on the self and others. In this instance, it is the knife that Anna had been carving meat with only moments before. After patching up Anna's wound, Marc turns the same knife on himself in a bid to understand her, making three superficial cuts to his forearm. "It doesn't hurt," Anna tells him. "No," a forlorn Marc replies. Later Anna will protect the creature she covets in her Kreuzberg apartment by attacking those she perceives as threats by fashioning weapons from domestic items: a broken wine bottle, a can of milk, a kitchen knife.

The latent horror of the everyday has a strong pedigree. In Polanski's *Repulsion* it is the uncooked rabbit that is left to decay in grim accordance with Carol's mental state. In Akerman's *Jeanne Dielman* (1975) it is the disruption of rigid routine that flags psychic disturbance. In Haneke's *The Seventh Continent* (1989) the cancelling of a newspaper subscription foreshadows a deathly change, the family's banal morning rituals destructively inverted before father, mother, and daughter commit suicide. Żuławski too recruits elements of the everyday to unsettling and expressive affect. In *Possession*, the apartment's orderliness deteriorates along with its occupants' psyches. Marc and Anna's unwashed clothing accumulates filth, and the couple often strain to be heard, yelling at one another over a series of abrasive sonic irritants: the clatter of china in the kitchen sink, the high whir of an electric knife, the incessant buzz of a meat grinder.

At the apogee of this madness, we see the family apartment in complete disarray, books and clothing strewn everywhere. Anna scoops a pile of clothing off the bedroom carpet and forces it into the kitchen fridge.

"What are you *doing*?!" Marc demands.

"I'm sorting out his things to take to the laundry."

Eyebrows arched, and mouth agape, Marc exhales, "I can do it myself!" His response isn't one of confusion, but of a man affronted by the insinuation that he has been derelict in his parental duty.

"But it's *my* job. I'm better at it," Anna replies, now haphazardly emptying the pantry, its contents spilling from her arms to the floor. Marc fidgets with and then replaces a slice of buttered bread he finds atop the refrigerator. The logic of the household has completely collapsed; here, the banal chores and domestic rituals that anchor us in the ordinary are turned on their head, the home adopting instead the lexicon of an absurd surrealist nightmare.

Bob is forgotten in the wake of Marc and Anna's breakup.

Bob is collateral damage in this tremendous fallout. Marc returns home after an absence of several weeks (he has been having what appears to be a nervous breakdown in a hotel room) to find the young boy alone. Bob sits on the floor of the messy apartment, surrounded by toys, clearly having been abandoned some time ago. Covered in jam, he tells his father: "Mummy said she'd be right back, but she never came." For much of the film, the child is either forgotten, left with surrogate carers, or recruited as a pawn in Marc's ploys for moral superiority over Anna during arguments.

As in other great horror renderings of the relationship breakdown melodrama, the trauma of familial dysfunction is inherited by the child. In David Cronenberg's *The Brood* (1979), young Candy bears the bites and scratches of what might be parental abuse, or the physical manifestation of her mothers' psychic demons. Danny, in Kubrick's *The Shining*, will likewise suffer ambiguous bruising at the impatient hand of an alcoholic father, or a malevolent apparition from a haunted hotel. In *Possession*, Bob's teacher informs Marc that the boy screams uncontrollably in his sleep, though here we are not offered a supernatural scapegoat. Bob is not the malevolent figure of films like *The Omen* (Donner 1976), *The Village of the Damned* (Rilla 1960), or *Ringu* (Nakata 1998). Nor is he held up as a symbol of hope in a brighter future. Bob is an innocent in a world corrupted by ordinary forces beyond his control—the collapse of the familial structure that can no longer be relied upon for stability and security.

'SHOOT THEM'

Possession is almost always in motion; in its full two hours, very seldom is the camera locked off. The camera's mobility does as much for the film's mood as the agitated performances it captures. At its most vital, Jaroszewicz's camera will charge down corridors, following characters or backing away from their advance. At other times, slow and deliberate tracking movement enlivens and makes strange otherwise undramatic moments. This mobility, often hand-held, does not equate to instability, however. Movement is fluid and precise, always in service of a given scene's temperament, the camera a phantom presence attune to the emotional turmoil it observes.

The mastery of *Possession*'s cinematography is perhaps most evident in the way the camera interacts with performances, anticipating and following characters in long takes as though propelled by the immediacy and gravity of their emotional states. Within the confines of interiors, the erratic movement of characters is hugged tightly by the camera, adding to an already claustrophobic tension. When Marc resolves to search through Anna's belongings, his eyes fixed in an expression of manic focus, the camera responds in kind. Fixing Marc in close-up, it tracks backward as Marc advances towards it, then circles clockwise around him, Marc pivoting on the spot into a rapid anti-clockwise spin against the grain of the camera's trajectory. This dance between camera and Marc is repeated later in the film, exaggerated and extended. Discovering the corpses in Anna's Kreuzberg apartment, Marc is suddenly overwhelmed. Absorbing this energy, the camera rapidly spirals around him several times in a dizzying whir, while he, gasping for air, reels in the alternate direction. Camera and performer unite in manic motion, the one contaminated by the other.

Conversations that American cinema has made us accustomed to experiencing in a shot / reverse-shot pattern, are in *Possession* covered in long takes, the camera slowly rotating around characters in whole or semi-circular movements. The meeting between Marc and his panel of employers at the beginning of the film is one such instance of a relatively undramatic narrative moment made dynamic. The camera traces great circles around its subjects, heightening the oddness of the moment it captures. This technique is repeated less conspicuously in the Café Einstein scene and again during the conversation between Anna and Detective Zimmerman, the camera making a slow semi-circle around static characters. Beyond the dynamism such movement adds, is the unison this orbicular pattern holds with the film's grander structure.

Also resonant is the suffocating proximity established during arguments. Domestic disputes usually relegated behind closed doors are not only made visible but are writ large. When the couple's quarrelling is captured in long shot, it is not unusual for Marc or Anna to be positioned close to the camera, the wide-angle lens stretching out the space behind them. However, it is the use of big close ups that force the viewer into an unnerving intimacy with physical and emotional conflict. Undoubtedly this contributed to Adjani's charge that with *Possession*, Żuławski had created 'emotional pornography.' The discharge of emotion, in the lexicon of pornography, is staged via "the principle of maximum visibility" (Williams 1989: 49), the camera looming perversely close as though to confirm the authenticity of the body beside itself in suffering.

In one such argument, immediately after Marc has beaten Anna, we alternate between extreme close-ups of each's perspective; Neill, his features contorted with grief and rage looks straight down the lens, before we cut to his perspective, Adjani addressing him / us, her face awash with tears and blood. The example *par excellence*, however, occurs during another argument when Marc demands Anna break off her affair over the phone. Here the perspective shifts from wide shot to extreme close-up without any adjustment of the camera. Instead Adjani, positioned impossibly close to the lens, need only lean back into the camera's field of vision, her anguished expression overwhelming the frame.

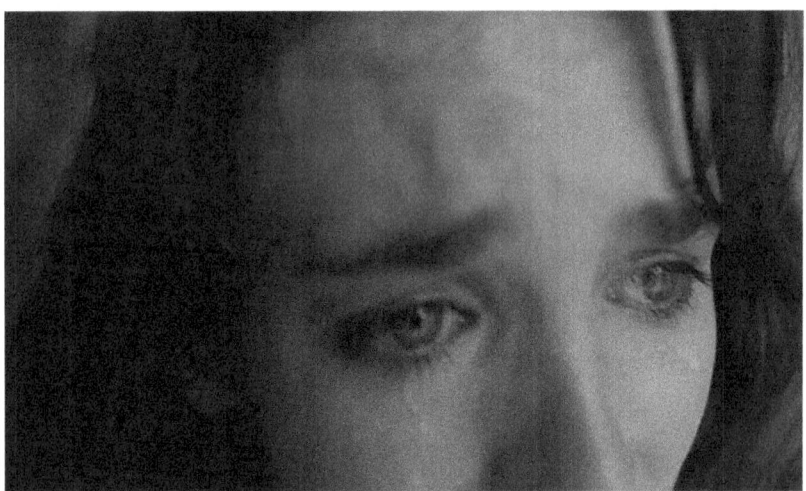

'Emotional pornography' – the discharge of emotions is staged for maximum visibility.

The occasional integration of extreme high and low angles similarly denaturalise our perspective on events. The camera gazes up from the floor as Anna grinds meat in the kitchen. At the other extreme, it gazes down from a vantage high above at Marc as he injures himself with the carving knife, and at the detective as he permits himself entry into Anna's Kreuzberg apartment. These shots are not motivated by any character's point of view; instead, they render familiar spaces and characters strange, contributing to the film's peculiar mood.

'WE ARE ALL THE SAME. BUT IN DIFFERENT WORDS. IN DIFFERENT BODIES. DIFFERENT VERSIONS'

Doubles are a recurrent phenomenon in Żuławski's films, both literally and metaphorically. In *The Third Part of the Night*, it is Michal's likeness who is murdered in his stead, and the pregnant stranger who bears an uncanny resemblance to his deceased wife. In *The Blue Note* (1991), characters discover puppets bearing their likeness within the film's mansion setting, which, at the film's end will announce their respective characters' fates. Żuławski also employs duality in a more abstracted sense, as in *The Devil*, when Jakub returns home after years in exile to find his best friend has taken over his life, or as in *The Public Woman* (1984) where amateur actress Ethel assumes the identity of a murdered woman.

In *Possession*, Żuławski's play with duality and division spans the literal and symbolic, informing the film to a degree that might best be described as kaleidoscopic; rearrange its components and new symmetries appear. Most overtly, we have the presence of doppelgängers: Helen appears as Anna's double, before the creature, mutated into its final form, reveals a more perfect incarnation of Marc. Interactions between characters are echoed and varied, opening parallels. At another level, Anna exhausts herself describing a psychic split—sisters faith and chance in violent contest for supremacy. And beneath this still, is Berlin, a city divided like Anna's identity, distorted like a funhouse mirror.

In the ostensibly realist world presented at *Possession*'s opening, the introduction of Helen is the first real clue that things might actually be askew. Marc meets her when he drops Bob off to school, shocked to discover that she bears a perfect resemblance to Anna, save for a different shade and style of hair, her eyes green rather than brown.

Always draped in white, Helen is Marc's idealised variant of Anna: placid, affectionate, reliable, and maternal. Stopping by the family apartment one evening requesting to speak to Anna, Helen seamlessly adapts to the role of mother in her absence, watching over Bob in the bath, and reading him a bedtime story. When Marc enters the kitchen to find Helen washing up, Żuławski enacts another doubling, this scene providing an uncanny echo of Marc and Anna's argument in the kitchen a few scenes prior. Helen has cleaned the kitchen we last saw strewn with mincemeat, the scene of Anna and Marc's self-mutilation. Anna's screams of "Excuse me!" at the husband constantly obstructing her path are here replaced by Helen's gentle request, "Excuse me," so she might reach the electric knife, wiping its blade clean. Just as Helen is to Anna, this exchange is refined and elevated; we have ascended a level of the film's winding structure.

Anna's doubling in Helen prefigures the monster's transformation into Marc's perfect double. It seems both Marc and Anna envision idealised versions of the other, finer than their flawed prototypes. While Anna actively cultivates Marc's double, giving birth to, and shaping it, Helen's status as Anna's refinement is more ambiguous. There is no indication that Marc has willed Helen into being in any conscious sense—he is alarmed to stumble upon her, and reacts with anger, assuming Anna is playing a cruel trick on him.

> Marc: "It's impossible... Have you ever seen my wife?"
>
> Helen: "Naturally. Every day of the school year."

Is Helen actually Anna's likeness, or have we adopted Marc's unreliable perspective? The film is ambiguous on this. Their likeness is not acknowledged by anyone else; Helen does not seem to be aware of it, and aside from Bob, no one else who knows Anna has any interactions with Helen. Being tucked into bed one night, Bob will ask his father whom he finds prettier, though we are left without any objective confirmation that this resemblance exists outside of Marc's subjectivity.

The possibility is left open then, that Helen's appearance as we perceive it is merely a projection of Marc's desires, fulfilling the qualities that Anna lacks. Helen will sleep with Marc, care for his son, keep his house in order, and in contrast to the ferocious quarrelling between the principal couple, the sole disagreement we witness between Marc and Helen remains measured and calm. At the same time, it is never settled that

Helen is not Anna's likeness, and given that multiple characters will bear witness to Anna's monster, it is entirely plausible that her doppelgänger exists within the world depicted.

Where doppelgängers in horror are typically a source of dread, Helen is a positive force, providing the care and sanctuary Bob has been lacking. The creature's transformation into Marc's likeness bears a more malevolent streak, though the nature of this malevolence is obscure. Like many of *Possession*'s mysteries, there are multiple ways we might interpret this dualism; is it the banal wish fulfilment of a dysfunctional relationship—the, *'if only he/she was some other way...'* daydream? Is it the purity and evil divide that Anna asserts more than once to be a false binary? Is it a further commentary on Berlin's physical and ideological divide—the split identity / monstrous other? Like sisters faith and chance "with their hands locked at each other's throats," Cold War Berlin is divided in hostile symbiosis. Who is on the *right* side of the Iron Curtain depends on which side one is standing.

To this last point, it is worth considering Keith J. Sanborn's reflections. Writing in 1983, Sanborn captures the peculiar phenomenon of Berlin's architecture:

> In Berlin, the double city, everything is halved and doubled—multiplied through division...East and West stand locked in a frozen stare, each the mirror image of the other. Each contemplates the spectacle of the other society; each remains oblivious that it is the society of the spectacle. In the East, ideology is merchandise; in the West, merchandise is ideology...Berlin is a city of doubles, divisions, dualities. An infinity of mirrors. (Sanborn 1983: 5)

Possession is also an infinity of mirrors, its components endlessly divisible. As Anna says, "goodness is only some kind of reflection upon evil."

'YOU, WITH YOUR YIN-YANG BALLS DANGLING FROM YOUR ZEN BRAIN?'

Scouring through Anna's belongings Marc finds a postcard from the Taj Mahal exposing her affair. It reads: "I've seen half of God's face here. The other half is you..." and is simply signed "Heinrich." Like Marc, we begin to formulate an impression of Heinrich before we see him, assembling from this message and the accumulation of new age literature nearby tell-tale fragments which might constitute an identity. Any inferences we can draw are surpassed, however, by the ludicrous caricature that opens the door when Marc arrives at Heinrich's apartment. Heinz Bennent's flamboyant performance really must be praised; Heinrich is painted as an absurd figure, his muscular bare chest exposed from his unbuttoned suit shirts—always simultaneously under and over-dressed—the theatrical inflation of his gestures, his impossibly earnest delivery of dialogue littered with proverbs.

Competing suitor, Heinrich.

While *Possession* is not lacking in exaggerated performances, Heinrich's presence is of a different register, possessing a camp sensibility. "Our situation is like a mountain lake we are trying to swim in, starting from different shores," Heinrich counsels, shortly before flooring Marc with an elaborate series of martial arts manoeuvres. Where other characters likewise maintain a serious delivery at odds with absurd situations, seldom are we prompted to meet this discrepancy with laughter. Conversely, Heinrich is invariably presented as an object for wonder and ridicule.

When Heinrich next appears, we have ascended a plane on the film's winding structure to see a reversal of this first encounter. This time the power dynamic has been inverted;

it is Heinrich who arrives unannounced, seeking information from Marc. Under the influence of God knows what, Heinrich's behaviour and speech are doubly bizarre. In the stairwell outside the family apartment, Heinrich spins, ricocheting off the walls. His eyes roll back into his head, and he addresses Marc with gesticulations that appear only partially under his control. At the same time, Bennent's heavily accented English has now been unshackled from any standard range of expression; he spills his cryptic aphorisms with a cadence and pitch that climbs and falls at irregular intervals.

Heinrich appears to offer Anna a pathway towards spirituality and freedom, yet this is shown up to be counterfeit. His divine encounters are chemically induced, and his words are emptied of meaning over time. Early in the film, Heinrich will claim to have opened Anna to herself. Later, we see Heinrich's vocabulary of liberation contort into contradiction, an attempt to possess her: "I'm the only one in your life who has rights on you, because I don't claim any." Each in their own ways, both Anna and Marc will wise up to Heinrich's posturing, rendering him powerless.

It is perhaps because Heinrich is so self-assured in his identity at the outset of the film that he has the furthest to fall. Marc takes a sadistic pleasure in informing Heinrich that he is not Anna's only extra-marital interest, a revelation that spurs Heinrich's unravelling. One feels Żuławski's schadenfreude also in this moment—directing a daydream in which the confidence of a cocksure sexual rival is shaken. Żuławski sees Heinrich vanquished by the couple—Anna wounds him after he discovers the monster. Marc finishes him off. After rejecting the now pathetic man's attempt at blackmail, Marc dispatches Heinrich by staging a drug overdose in the restroom of a dingy bar. If this is Żuławski's waking fantasy of recompense for being wronged by Braunek's suitor, it, like everything else is turned up to 11. Ultimately, Heinrich will die debased and humiliated, drowning "in a flood of shit."

'WHAT IS THIS, A JOKE?'

Heinrich is one element of humour in the film, but there are others. Marc's interactions with the shadowy organization he works for is one such thread. The detective agency he employs to trace Anna is another. These men in suits subplots are deliberately thin, the figures that populate them empty caricatures lifted from genre movies. Marc meets with his employers, one of whom sports an eyepatch, in the corner of an absurdly vast and otherwise empty room. A handheld camera tracks around them in great circles, as they each take turns at interrogating him. We aren't told what Marc's assignment abroad was, and in the great scheme of the narrative it doesn't seem to matter. Cryptic fragments of dialogue suggest some kind of espionage mission: "What time did you meet him?"; "How many vials did he take with him?"; "Does our subject still wear pink socks?"

Late in the film, one of these panellists finds Marc on the Lohmühlen Bridge—right on the Western border of the Wall—observing a dead dog floating in the canal below. What follows is a bizarre exchange of dialogue delivered in earnest; generic markers of the spy film are interspersed with poetic imagery that seems swollen with meaning. Adding to the absurdity, it is later revealed that the same employer has been their pink sock-wearing subject all along, a double-agent tasked with spying on himself.

This entire narrative thread, it will turn out, is a tease. The pink socks and dead dogs are merely cyphers to which there is no solution in a mystery that doubles back on itself. While Cold War era Berlin provided a backdrop for a great many serious espionage thrillers replete with double-crossing emissaries, Żuławski is poking fun here. The pink socks, Żuławski has expressed in interviews, are a joke at the expense of Eastern authorities striving to be Western. For Żuławski, this is the stuff of Polish humour, more abstract than Western audiences are accustomed to. "I don't know what that means...but it makes me laugh," Żuławski has said of the pink sock conspiracy. "I see many people who are devastated by not knowing very well what they saw, and they do not dare believe that it is funny at times" (qtd. in Bonitzer & Toubiana 1981: 42).

One would be harder pressed to not find comedy in the detective agency subplot. That an international spy would approach a private detective for aid tracking his wife is already absurd. The agency's methods, however, amount to something like a series of *Monty Python* sketches. Addressing detective Zimmerman at his office, Marc awkwardly explains "I would like you to follow my, ah- wife for a few days." "Of course!" Zimmerman replies. Swivelling his chair around to the filing cabinet beside him, Zimmerman thinks aloud "Wives, wives, wives, wives..." as his hand dances down the stack searching for the corresponding drawer. It's not Zimmerman, but another gumshoe, played by Carl Duering, who is sent to trace Anna. His efforts are unsubtle, chasing her down the streets to her Kreuzberg address. When Anna reaches her door, the detective continues to the next floor, comically running on the spot to give the illusion of being further away. The coast cleared, the detective brings his splayed palm to his chest in a theatrically inflated gesture signalling the cost of this physical expenditure.

Where Anna's monster, and the marital conflict even at its most extreme moments are treated gravely, Żuławski also inserts throwaway moments of playful surrealism. Riding the U-Bahn, a drunk reaches into Anna's grocery bag, helping himself to a banana; upon seeing the Kreuzberg apartment in flames, an elderly woman on the street leaps and whirls ecstatically; Margie, hobbling into the family apartment with her leg in a cast and her arms loaded up with shopping bags, collapses in the kitchen for no apparent reason. These comedic flourishes certainly contribute to *Possession*'s strange atmosphere. Rather than jarring with the severity of other scenes, they are elements of Żuławski's world-building, recognisable but made strange.

'BECAUSE YOU SAY "I" FOR ME'

To talk about the representation of women in *Possession* is complicated. On the one hand, we could read *Possession* as a misogynistic story about a neurotic woman whose selfishness and infidelity tears her family apart. Through this lens, Anna is but another in a long line of cinematic representations of the hysterical female, in this instance so caught up in her own desires, that she forgets her child altogether. Alternately, *Possession* might be interpreted as a feminist chant—the tale of a woman who turns away from the oppressive bonds of marriage and family in the pursuit of self-fulfilment and pleasure, like a deranged retelling of Ibsen's *A Doll's House*.

Neither extreme of this spectrum feels satisfactory. "Look, Marc. That woman is crazy. We have to do something!" Heinrich implores towards the end of the film. But these words are spoken into a world that is mad; Heinrich is far from stable, and by this point in the film Marc has well and truly ventured through the looking glass. In Żuławski's universe, hysteria is not a female malady, but a symptom of existence—it can afflict anyone and everyone. Conversely, where Ibsen's Nora makes her decisive exit at the end of the play, having explained her grievances to Torvald, Anna is neither resolute nor articulate in her protest. Just as she periodically erupts into and then disappears from the family apartment, Anna seems torn between competing responsibilities and desires.

Possession aligns us with Marc's point of view; very few scenes occur independent of his presence. However, this physical alignment does not equate to an endorsement of his perspective. Marc is not painted as the honourable party with whom to wholeheartedly empathise, rather, he is shown to be emotionally and physically abusive to Anna on several occasions. Further, while Helen may appeal to Marc's desires—both as carer and source of intimacy—she does not exist simply to acquiesce to those desires. When Marc complains that he is "at war against women," Helen unemotively dismisses his barrage of misogynistic generalisations: "There is nothing in common among women except menstruation," she tells him, ultimately branding his outlook as "pathetic." That Marc's bruised masculinity is so gracefully disarmed underscores its foolishness. At the same time, Helen's presence as the saintly double to Anna's adulteress evokes something of Freud's Madonna-whore complex, the one stepping in to cater to Marc's ego in the absence of the other.

Attempting to classify *Possession*'s treatment of gender as wholly anything would be a reductive exercise. Just as Lars von Trier's *Antichrist* (2009) garnered both criticism and praise for its perceived misogyny and feminism respectively, *Possession* lends itself to varied responses. While I have no intention of arguing its status as a feminist masterpiece, I feel equally compelled to counter charges that it is downright misogynistic. I will return to this question in Chapter 5, when I consider the film's resurgence, having found a substantial female fan base,. However, for now, I want to point to what I perceive to be an important element in this regard: Anna's self-expression.

Throughout the film Anna struggles to convey her needs and desires both to herself and the men who seek to control her. Often her expression amounts to bursts of fragmented speech, guttural moans, and screams. What is significant, though, is that she has a voice.

Anna's voice is heard most consistently in a home movie, shot by Heinrich and left as a package on Marc's doorstep. We watch this film within a film, with Marc, first taking his perspective—the grainy images flickering on a home projector, before a transition takes us into the film he is watching. The first segment takes place within a ballet studio where

Anna is teaching a class of pre-pubescent girls. Anna turns her attention sadistically to one pupil in particular. The girl gasps and moans in agony as Anna forces her to hold an excruciating pose, before moving on to praise the next student who by comparison is barely trying. Agonised now at the injustice of Anna's misplaced affection, the tortured student, mouth agape, runs crying from the studio slamming the door behind her.

This event prompts Anna to monologue: "From now on, she'll know how much righteous anger and sheer will she has in her to say 'I. I can do as well, I can be better, I'm the best!' Only in this case can she become a success. Nobody taught me that." Anna sighs, and turns directly to address Heinrich's camera: "Well that's why I'm with you. Because you say 'I' for me. Because you say 'I' for me." This is a curious and confronting moment. Within the diegesis, Anna is addressing Heinrich, and now simultaneously addressing Marc, yet her accusatory gaze cast directly down the lens implicates us also, breaking the fourth wall.

Anna's look down the lens makes Heinrich, Marc, and the viewer complicit.

The next segment of Heinrich's home movie observes Anna sat on the floor, presumably at his apartment. In a series of tight shots, she rocks back and forth on the spot, sweating and agitated. Desperately, Anna is trying to articulate herself; a feverish monologue expels from her in fits and starts, the jerkiness of which is emphasised by jump cuts. An extract from this monologue is below.

> I recognise the self who has just done something horrible like a sister I've casually met in the street – 'Hello, sister!'...It's like those two sisters are faith and chance. My faith can't exclude chance, but my chance can't explain faith. My faith didn't allow me to wait for chance and chance didn't give me enough faith. Well, and then I read that private life is a stage, only I play in it many parts that are smaller than me and yet, I still play them. I suffer, I believe, I am. But at the same time, I know there's a third possibility, like cancer or madness, but cancer or madness contort reality. The possibility I'm talking about *pierces* reality.

Anna's full monologue touches on several other subjects—her guilt over betraying Marc, her fear of herself, even the nature of good and evil. Though fraught with the incoherence of a stream of troubled consciousness, these monologues strike me as revelatory moments of self-realisation. Elsewhere in the film, both Marc and Heinrich will say 'I' for Anna, speaking *for* her in selfish attempts to press her to their will. In the 8mm home movie, by contrast, Anna is able to speak about her experience and perception uninterrupted. In doing so, Anna articulates her own sense of identity, albeit fragmented.

Here and elsewhere in the film, Anna seems tormented by a split in her psyche. Her struggle is evoked in the imagery of two sisters, "faith" and "chance," imagery that becomes recurrent. In the following scene, when Anna attempts to explain her experience to Marc, she describes the sisters as competing impulses violently battling for dominance, until sister faith is miscarried during the film's central U-Bahn sequence. Thereafter, faith (that which becomes the creature) is described as something that needs to be protected "like a child." Anna will kill those who try to take it from her. But sister faith is faith in what exactly? Love? A future? Perhaps it is simply *faith*—pure divinity. Żuławski will not say, and I do not profess to know. Żuławski makes his anti-theoretical stance clear during interviews, and so I trust that like the film's other mysteries, these moments are intended to be experienced rather than decoded.

The other theme I want to touch on in these monologues is that of suffering. Of course, *Possession* is a film about anguish, but here suffering is intrinsically linked to the 'I' that Anna articulates. It is only through the experience of suffering, Anna suggests, that her student will discover the 'I' within her. Identity and suffering are linked again in the second monologue: "I suffer, I believe, I am." Descartes's cogito is here refigured, suffering preceding the capacity for the self. I take the film's broader structure, its repetitions and differences, to represent an ascent out of suffering. If our characters begin in the material world, at odds with themselves and one another, gradually, via Żuławski's winding formal pattern, they move closer to something like self-realisation and divinity.

2. METAPHYSICAL

THE CREATURE

Anna's coveted secret.

We are almost halfway through the film when we first see the creature. It is discovered by the detective, concealed in the bathroom of Anna's Kreuzberg apartment: an indistinct shape, bloody and glistening. A single eye gleams back at him from the darkness. Our next view of it is more complete, and for that, more disturbing. Zimmerman will see it, peering into Anna's bedroom. The green sheets and yellow walls are stained with blood. On the middle of the mattress is a hideous shape: an elongated head meets a bulbous heart-like torso from which tentacles have sprouted. Drenched in blood, the creature looks like a giant wad of breathing viscera. The lethargic mass slowly raises its head for a moment to meet Zimmerman's disturbed gaze, its tentacles flopping about its side like intestines. "He's very tired," Anna tells Zimmerman. "He made love to me all night." An elevated wide shot reveals the timber floor is slick with a grotesque mixture of fluids: red, white, green. Anna concludes: "He's still unfinished, you know."

Heinrich is the next to see it, in a dark corner of the Kreuzberg apartment. Obscured somewhat by distance and darkness, it appears very much like a man, naked, bloodied, its head slumped forward. It has grown larger, the chest has filled out, and the tentacles look like arms resting by its side. A close-up reveals its face, its head elongated like a blood drenched phallus, its emerald green eyes shine, and a slit mouth opens and closes with labored breaths. This vision is enough to strike Heinrich temporarily blind, as though his visual sense, so overwhelmed, retreated entirely.

Our final view of the creature before its transformation is complete comprises perhaps the film's most scandalous image. Moonlight through the windows of Margie's house illuminates Anna's naked body splayed in bed as the creature fucks her hungrily. By now its head and torso are humanoid, though tracing its back as it arches reveals its lower body culminates in a great long tentacle that thrusts inside Anna, eliciting orgasmic screams, its other tentacles wrapped around her arms and legs. Our shock and awe at this audacious imagery is reflected on Marc's face as he approaches fascinated and terrified. "Almost!" Anna repeats, staring desperately at her husband. Like everything in Żuławski's film, this "almost" is doubled; the almost of sexual satisfaction is the almost of the creature's final form.

Crafted by the legendary Carlo Rambaldi, the monster inspires dread in those that see it, often veiled in darkness. Gruesomely and painfully evacuated from Anna's body, it mutates over time, becoming more humanoid. But even with this nod to the genre's visual effects, the monster is still Other. Where in *Invasion of the Body Snatchers* (Kaufman 1978) and *The Thing* (Carpenter 1982), monstrous evil is an insidious force, imitating human form to preserve its own existence, in *Possession* the creature is borne of the human psyche, its transformation willed by its creator. Where in *Rosemary's Baby* and *Eraserhead*, the monstrous offspring causes fear and disgust in its mother, in *Possession*, Anna's progeny evolves, maturing into an incestuous partner.

The monster's meaning, like its shape, is ill-defined. Is it a positive image, something Anna cultivates to fulfill her unmet sexual desires? Is it the physical manifestation of Anna's distress and torment? Is it a mess of psychic weight that had to be expelled once she could carry it no longer? Is it the political malevolence of the communist bloc that Żuławski sought to critique, finally having infiltrated the West? Or perhaps the profane seed of God, Anna miscarrying after her pained encounter with the icon of Christ crucified? It is worth remembering that even during the shooting process, the monster's origins were in flux, with alternate and conflicting representations of its creation abandoned during the shooting process.

Marc follows Anna into madness.

With this, I think it's important to stress that the monster ought not to be taken as having a singular or absolute meaning. Multiple readings are available, often at the same time, and it seems Żuławski himself had never entirely settled on its significance, describing it in varied ways. In his director's commentary, Żuławski describes Anna as giving birth to something "like a cancer" (Żuławski 2000). Elsewhere, he has extrapolated, likening this evacuation of something evil from the self to the dangers of political and ideological rhetoric; once expressed, the "blah blah" of ideology takes on a life of its own, and one that has the potential to kill en masse (Bird 2009a). At the same time, Żuławski makes clear the openness of its interpretability, stating: "I dare you to give a coherent explanation of the thing. I dare you to. I dare myself to give a coherent explanation of evil" (qtd. in Bird 2009a).

'I'M READY TO UNDERSTAND WHATEVER THERE IS, BUT IT DOESN'T LOOK LIKE IT MAKES MUCH SENSE'

If the trajectory of *Possession*'s characters is away from the fleshy, bodily, and material towards the transcendental, part of this journey is also away from the confines of rationality. It is interesting to consider the way the narrative moves from a mystery plot, to one where the dictates of reason become less and less important. Initially *Possession* presents Anna like an enigma that must be investigated and solved. Marc will follow clues (a postcard, an 8mm film), interrogate witnesses (Anna, Heinrich, Margie), and call on external resources (the detective agency) for assistance. This approach is one geared towards mastery, where resolution means a containment of meaning through rational explanation. But it is a futile approach because Anna's crisis resists control and containment. The more Anna struggles to articulate her experience in communicable terms, the more tormented she becomes. Likewise, Marc's demands that she "restore order," and respect propriety, only elevate his frustration and anguish. In this way, madness, for lack of a better word (that which "pierces reality"), is conceived of as a radical form of freedom in *Possession* once one ceases trying to resist its clutches and surrenders to its surreal logic.

After several fruitless arguments, Marc comes to realise that to understand Anna is to adopt her language; that is, the lexicon of her folie. Żuławski (2000) has described Marc's attempts to do so as akin to a parent speaking with a child: "You say *'oh yes, so this is the monster who comes every night from under the bed, and I understand, we will do something about it.'*" This is not to suggest that Anna needs to be coddled, but rather that when one ceases trying to impose a rational framework and engages with the surreal logic dictated by the situation, there can be a productive shift in perspective.

Though we see glimpses of Marc's mentality shifting over the course of the film, the tipping point comes when he finally enters Anna's secret apartment in Kreuzberg, now abandoned. Inside he discovers the remnants of Anna's murders: the hallway is lined with bulky garbage bags, the fridge packed with severed limbs ridden with flies. A shocked laugh gives way to retching as though Marc were about to vomit. Instead, his eyes draw wide and his whole body begins to spin in dizzying circles while he hyperventilates and heaves. Screaming, he bursts onto the apartment balcony to regain composure, a maniacal grin transforms his features, his eyes ablaze with madness. In this moment, the body and psyche are overwrought, a mental state expressed not only in Neill's performance, but in the film's style. In what Daniel Bird (2012) has described as "the most succinct cinematic representation of 'cosmic horror,'" Korzyński's score erupts into a chaotic storm of percussive instruments underscored by a low cello shivering in staccato, and Jaroszewicz's camera whirls in frenetic counter motion to Neill's movement.

In Cronenberg's *The Brood*, when Frank plans to rescue his daughter from the clutches of his estranged wife, Nola, he tells her: "I want us to understand each other...I want to be with you, wherever you go." Frank is feigning. Moments later he will strangle Nola to death. *Possession*'s Marc, on the other hand, means to follow his wife headlong into the fold.

'HOW COULD YOU FIND ME?' A TRAGEDY OF REMARRIAGE

Marc's assenting to Anna's madness sees the shift in the narrative. Hereafter, Marc's path is clear; he will do everything in his power to aid his wife. With this, the film's pace escalates rapidly; in its remaining half hour Marc murders Heinrich, blows up Anna's apartment to conceal evidence of her crimes, hides Margie's corpse, wages an attack on the police who mean to infiltrate Anna's hideout, narrowly escapes from a severe motorcycle accident, and reunites with Anna in the climactic staircase sequence. More importantly, however, it is Marc's choice to discard attempts at controlling Anna, and to surrender to her folie, that shifts the trajectory of the pair away from conflict to co-operation and paves the way for their romantic reconnection.

As church bells toll in the distance, Marc heaves his broken and bloodied frame up the winding staircase as far as he can before collapsing. Dashing footsteps can be heard behind him. Spying Anna below, Marc pleads for her to run away, but she ignores this command, tracing the banister with her hands as she ascends. Another figure follows, for the moment obscured. "How could you find me?" Marc wonders aloud. "How could I not?" Anna beams: "I wanted to show it to you. It is finished now." Having caught up to Marc, Anna presents him with the creature, now fully transformed, Marc's perfect replica.

Marc raises his pistol towards his likeness, the latter regarding him with a mixture of fascination and confusion. It is this gesture that triggers gunfire from the stairwell below as Marc's pursuers unleash a torrent of bullets. Injured, Anna strains to adjust her bloodsoaked body so she might embrace Marc, a laborious and intimate gesture. The pair exchange a gruesome kiss, and with a final agonising motion, Anna draws a pistol behind her back to shoot herself and Marc, who rests beneath her.

It is of course deeply tragic that this couple, seemingly incapable of coexisting peacefully, find their ideal in their re-creation of each other. If Marc has found his ideal Anna in the figure of Helen—warm, calm, and motherly—it is revealed that regardless of all that has gone before, Anna's ideal is in Marc. In spite of her infidelity with Heinrich, her desperation to escape the home, and her professed repulsion towards her husband, it is Marc that she desires, reborn and sculpted, coveted and killed for. For Żuławski, the monster's transformation was inevitable. Anna could not possibly have re-created anyone else: "It's a love story. The whole thing...between people who cannot connect, comprehend, understand, *be* together" (Żuławski 2000). It is even more tragic, then, that this couple, incapable of connecting, are impossibly reconciled in their obliteration.

To me, this reunion plays like a tragic inversion of Stanley Cavell's (2003) concept of the "comedy of remarriage" in Hollywood screwball comedies like *It Happened One Night* (Capra 1934) and *His Girl Friday* (Hawks 1940). Taking his cue from Ibsen, Cavell imagines remarriage comedies as a kind of response to the problem posed by Nora at the end of *A Doll's House* when she tells Torvald that in order for them to reconcile, both would have to undergo miraculous change. For Cavell, in remarriage comedies, romantic couples struggle for a mutual understanding, a "reconciliation so profound as to require the metamorphosis of death and revival, the achievement of a new perspective on existence" (2003: 19). Where in the comedic register, the reconciliation of the romantic couple occurs through a metaphorical transfiguration, in its tragic form, the capacity for the couple's mutual acknowledgment is necessitated by extremity, the metamorphosis of death and revival literalised.

Possession is not alone in its tragic formulation of the remarriage plot. Consider Liliana Cavani's *The Night Porter* (1974), for instance. Recognising that their erotic reunion cannot be sustained outside of the extreme context in which it was forged, ex-SS officer Max and ex-concentration camp prisoner Lucia deliver themselves to their enemies, to be gunned down together at sunrise. Similarly, Jean Rollin's *The Night of the Hunted* (1980) ends with the romantic reunion of a couple whose reciprocity of consciousness is dependent upon mutual brain death. In George Sluizer's *The Vanishing* (1988), Rex can only be reunited with his fiancée, who inexplicably disappeared years prior, when he consents to undergo the same treatment at the hands of the man who abducted her.

Marc and Anna together at last in death.

In *Possession*, as in these other tragic formulations of the remarriage plot, we see a Bataillean vision of the erotic; the individual is paradoxically caught between a desire to transcend their separateness from the other, and the knowledge that transcendence is impossible: necessitating the dissolution of the individual. Tragedies of remarriage offer a cathartic vision, albeit fleeting, of what Georges Bataille describes as our human yearning "to bring into a world founded on discontinuity all the continuity such a world can sustain" (1986: 19). To reconnect with Anna, Marc joins her in her madness. Such a heightened state can only be sustained for so long, however, before the world closes in. The pair are romantically reunited in death upon the Palais staircase.

THE LADDER OF PROFANE ASCENT

> Satan from hence now on the lower stair
> That scaled by steps of gold to Heaven gate
> Looks down with wonder at the sudden view
> Of all this world at once.
> John Milton, *Paradise Lost* (iii 540)

Żuławski, like Grotowski[3] held the biblical image of Jacob's ladder to be a significant influence in his work. Described in the Book of Genesis as a ladder linking Heaven and Earth, Jacob's ladder has been broadly interpreted to be a conduit between life and death, or an ascetic path to divinity. The ascetic reading, famously promulgated by John Climacus's *The Ladder of Divine Ascent* sees the ladder as a grueling climb away from the world and the body's earthly desires through cultivation of the virtues, to at last commune with God. In William Blake's painting, *Jacob's Dream*, the ladder is envisioned as an immense spiral staircase ascending to the heavens, seemingly absorbed by the sun. In *Possession*, it is the grand winding staircase of the Palais, the glass ceiling blown out in white light that gives the gives the vast room an unearthly illumination.

Jacob's Ladder – *William Blake c. 1805*
© *The Trustees of the British Museum.*

Marc, broken and bloodied will not complete the ascent, nor will Anna. Instead, it is Marc's double, divine and profane, who will escape via an open window on the roof. Unlike Anna's counterpart in Helen, we hardly see enough of Marc's double to gauge his character, though what we are privy to in this scene suggests a charismatic malevolence. At the top of the stairs, he meets a woman we have not seen before who is mesmerized by his presence and will aid his escape.[4] The creature addresses her with a slow deliberateness that is seductive; placing Marc's pistol in her hands he guides her aim to the stairwell below where police are waiting, gently commanding her with wide eyes and a broad and monstrous grin to "shoot them." Releasing a round, the woman's eyes flash, her face flushed with ecstasy. With a wave of his splayed fingers, the creature tacitly commands the woman to help hoist him so he might reach the ceiling window. Before escaping, he outstretches an arm, addressing the shooters below. "How do you want to finish it?" he calls, before climbing out. Żuławski (2000) claims he had intended for this scene to continue further, with Marc's double walking the building's roof, surveying the city below, "floating like the Devil above this corrupted, strange, divided city." According to Żuławski (2000), it was only time and budget constraints that had prevented this footage from being shot, yet notably this scene does not exist in the screenplay.

The film is edging towards its apocalyptic crescendo. Żuławski's apocalyptic sensibility had already been established in *The Third Part of the Night* and *The Devil*, both of which refer to the Book of Revelation. *Possession* will end with an apocalypse, signaled by an intrusion of light and sound. Just as the everyday aspects of *Possession* were inspired by personal experience, so too is this. "I was born from an apocalypse," Żuławski explains in his director's commentary, "I was born in a city in Poland in 1940, and my sister died from hunger and my mother and my father were the only surviving people from a huge family...so for me everything commences- begins with an apocalypse" (Żuławski 2000). What are we to make of the fact that it is not divine goodness that ascends the ladder, but divine evil, come to herald the apocalypse? Perhaps we ought to remember that Satan too was an angel.

'HOW DO YOU WANT TO FINISH IT?'

> I saw Bergman's film *Scenes from a Marriage* – it's very good, but bizarrely unfinished, unsatisfactory by the end, inconclusive. – Andrzej Żuławski (qtd. in Thrower & Bird 2003: 71)

Like *Possession*, *Scenes from a Marriage* (Bergman 1973) charts the deterioration of a relationship, its central couple wrenched apart and reunited over the course of a decade. Johan and Marianne seem incapable of letting one another go in any final sense; their saga doesn't really end, only Bergman's telling of it. At the film's (or miniseries) conclusion, Johan and Marianne are divorced from one another, and married to others. Clandestinely they rendezvous, we are told, "In the Middle of the Night in a Dark House Somewhere in the World." Whether they will, or *can*, ever conclusively sever their connection is a question beyond the scope of Bergman's *Scenes*. But for tonight, they are together, in each other's arms.

Possession's conclusion leaves no such space for ambiguity. Żuławski pushes his tale of marriage and divorce to the point of no return. In the film's final scene, Bob sits at a grand dining table in Helen's apartment, the various breakfast elements stretched out before him surrounded by scores of toy soldiers. The doorbell chimes and Helen requests that Bob answer it, but the child steadfastly refuses. "Don't open," he cautions, then commands. "But I want to," Helen replies with a playful pat to Bob's head, approaching the door. "Don't open!" Bob repeats over and over with growing desperation. Running up the apartment stairs, his echoed plea ceases only when he throws himself face down into the bathtub full of water. Korzyński's melancholy piano refrain returns, though it is now in contest with the drone of sirens and bomber planes. We leave Bob laying prone underwater, cutting to Helen at the door, for a moment afraid. The light flickers as bombs fall, and behind the door we can see the creature's silhouette pressing against frosted glass awaiting entry. The camera zooms in on Helen's face, porcelain white; her expression now impassive is periodically veiled in darkness and then illuminated brightly by the gleam of off-screen explosions. The image is haunting; those deathly green eyes stare straight down the lens at us. A final over-exposed burst of light, a final crash on the soundtrack, and then a final blackness.

This finality is crucial. For Bergman, "can two people spend a life together?" is a proposition without resolution. If *Scenes from a Marriage* is a question mark, in this regard, Żuławski's *Possession* is the period that precludes further discourse. Żuławski erases the material world in order to transcend it. I have discussed the film's formal architecture as an ascension away from the material world, as its imperfect characters strive for the impossibility of unison. *Possession* opened with Marc returning home to his family. Here, at the film's end, we see this event renewed and elevated upon the film's spiral structure of perpetual return and revision. Our ascent is complete.

FOOTNOTES

3. Jacob's ladder had featured in the central sequence of Grotowski's performance *Akropolis* which premiered in 1962. The ladder remained an influence on Grotowski's thinking throughout his career. His final phase of research, 'Ritual Arts' or 'Art as vehicle' which commenced in 1986, was fundamentally informed by a vertical framework. As Laster explains: "In discussing this work Grotowski alludes to the powerful image of Jacob's ladder—a struggle to rise from the level of the purely physical to the psychophysical and, ultimately, the spiritual" (2016: 93).
4. The young blonde with a club foot is Sara, a ghostly remnant from an earlier version of the script. See Chapter 2 for details.

Chapter 4: 'If You Had Only Seen What I Saw!' – *Possession*'s Reception

> ...people have this curious tendency when dealing with art or so-called art that they become rigid...They want to keep the serious things apart from the vulgar and the frivolous etc. And they're wrong! – Andrzej Żuławski (qtd. in The Ferroni Brigade 2012)

At a conference, not too long ago, a certain gatekeeping Canadian film critic took umbrage to my placing Jean Rollin and Liliana Cavani in the same sentence. The gist of his grievance was that Rollin was a pornographer while Cavani was an artist. The problem with insisting upon such boundaries is that they rarely hold under scrutiny. *The Night Porter* is an exceptional film. But one needn't squint hard to see a Nazisploitation flick with a budget.

This perceived necessity to quarantine highbrow from lowbrow has always amused me, but it's also what makes *Possession*'s sliding status between these two poles so fascinating. If—at least as far as critics are concerned—horror is lowbrow for appealing to the senses, and art cinema is highbrow for being cerebral, then what were they to make of *Possession*? What were audiences to do with this strange object caught between the material and metaphysical, art cinema and genre movie? Like its protagonists, spattered in blood and sprawled upon a metaphorical Jacob's ladder, *Possession* is splayed awkwardly in-between. At one end of the spectrum, the film would premiere in competition at the world's leading art cinema festival. At the other, it would be embroiled with a moral panic that led to charges of obscenity.

Cannes

Possession premiered, in competition for the Palme d'Or, at Cannes on the 25th of May, 1981. Also in contention for the top prize were Michael Cimino's *Heaven's Gate*, Hugh Hudson's *Chariots of Fire*, and Juliet Berto's *Neige*, amongst several others. However, it was Żuławski's mentor, Andrzej Wajda, who would win, with *Man of Iron*. This film, a follow-up to *Man of Marble* (1977) told of the rise of Solidarity and the very recent

Gdańsk shipyard strike. There was some hushed speculation on the Promenade la Croisette that Wajda's film had won for diplomatic reasons—the festival coincided with election of France's socialist president, François Mitterrand. A less cynical majority praised Wajda's film as the worthy winner, adding that its only real competition was István Szabó's *Mephisto*.

For the Golden Palm, *Possession* seemed an unlikely contender and inevitably, it ruffled some feathers. Sam Neill reflects: "The film was a sensation at Cannes and predictably was adored by some and loathed by others" (personal communication, March 14, 2019). Amongst the adoring was Max Tessier. Writing for *Image et Son – La Revue de Cinema*, Tessier (1981a: 22) described *Possession* as the "fantastical avatar of a mystical, genius of a filmmaker who gives meaning back to the word 'cinema.'" In *Lumière du cinéma*, he doubled down, declaring Żuławski a "new master" in the baroque vein of Welles, Fellini, and Kubrick (Tessier 1981b). Hubert Niogret of *Positif* was similarly impressed by the boldness Żuławski's style, stating: "It is rare and exceptional for a filmmaker to dare to push what cinema is capable of expressing to such limits" (1981: 115).

Though critics offered due respect to *Possession*'s technical precision, many were less fond of its excesses. While Annette Insdorf (1981: 27) noted the titters of American critics over the film's immoderation, and Philip French of *The Observer* described *Possession* as a "lunatic German film" resembling "a demented cross between *Private Lives* and *Alien*" (1981: 31), others found the film genuinely disturbing. Writing for *Le Monde*, Jean de Baroncelli (1981) described this "Dark, nauseating, and dizzying" film as having "traumatised the Festival." For Claude Baignères, while Żuławski's and Adjani's talents were undoubtedly masterful, "enough is enough," and Pierre Montaigne cautioned audiences that *Possession* was "one of the most traumatic shocks of his long career" (qtd. in Fortier 1981: 39).

Perhaps most resolute in his disdain was Pascal Bonitzer of *Cahiers du cinéma* who dedicated two pages to excoriating the film for wallowing in senseless violence and hollow symbolism. Bonitzer seems to relish in describing the viscera he ostensibly abhors, the "huge clots" of blood, the "deluge of vomit," the "primitive and filthy matter." After describing Anna's miscarriage in the U-Bahn ("Adjani disgorges like a snail"), Bonitzer suggests that viewers would do well to follow her lead, "to purge oneself of all the cursed juices, of all the infamous substances with which the film is engorged" (1981: 30).

To this end, the jury (and it should be noted, most critics) disagreed; Adjani would receive the prize for Best Actress—the only actress to date who would win this award for two films in the one festival—for her roles in *Possession* and James Ivory's *Quartet*. This decision too seemed to house an inherent contradiction, Adjani's performances as antithetical as sister faith and sister chance. In *Quartet* Adjani is the beautiful *ingénue* in a quaint albeit bleak chamber play, in *Possession* she screams, vomits, and exorcises her innermost self. But if Anna was undergoing a psychic split between two warring identities, *Possession* too would be pitched against itself—the US release, recut by a team of outsourced editors would become something like an evil twin.

THE US CUT

> They opened the film on Halloween in New York, in one movie house. I went to see it, and I realised what they had done. They had cut out, basically cut out the interaction of the characters that was basically a psychological interaction in favour of winnowing the film down to a kind of horror story...it was just amputated, it was dead.
> – Frederic Tuten (qtd. in Iatrou & Morgan 2019)

The cut released for the US market is truly an abomination. In a scathing assessment for *The New York Times*, Vincent Canby lambasted the film on several fronts, not least for being nonsensical. One can almost forgive Canby's verdict, considering the extent to which the film he saw had been butchered beyond recognition. But only almost. Noting reports that viewers at Cannes had found the film to be traumatising, Canby suggests that "New York audiences may be reduced to helpless laughter." While he acknowledges that part of this discrepancy might be attributable to the radically reduced running time, he reasons that "it's possible to see that *Possession* would look fairly preposterous at any length" (1983: C10).

The critique is unfair, but it's doubtful that Canby could imagine just how different the two cuts are. The changes do not just amount to shaving a two-hour running time to make the film more attractive for a US audience; the film has been dramatically altered. Thirty-seven minutes are missing from the original. Scenes are re-ordered and intercut with other scenes rendering an already obtuse and enigmatic film unintelligible. Attempts to condense screen-time without losing dialogue means scenes are re-edited with such ineptitude that fundamental spatial relationships are no longer clear; the effect is disorienting. Korzyński's score has been almost entirely replaced with sound choices that range from odd to absurd. Effects, both sonic and visual have been added with no apparent motivation.

Take, for instance, the reveal of Anna in bed with her tentacled lover. In the US cut, Marc's return to Margie's house is accompanied by what might as well be the explosion of a stock sound effects library. In a scene lasting two-and-a-half minutes, we hear a cacophony of noises including, but certainly not limited to: thunder and wind from an absent storm, bursts of 'ominous' children's laughter, an anonymous male moaning sound, a choral rendition of 'Bah Bah Black Sheep,' rats squeaking, a foreboding Latin choir, and a wide assortment of other atonal synthetic sounds someone likely found on a discounted 'spooky' soundboard. This scene ends with a freeze frame close-up of Marc's face, which is then solarized save for his eyes which glow red, before a rostrum effect zooms in.

While these decisions are likely attributable to the distributor's want to boost its genre appeal to horror fans, crucially, not all of the changes are superficial. Some have significant impacts on the film's meaning. For instance, an early scene when Marc is awakened by a telephone call from Anna telling him that she is downtown and needs some time to think is radically different in the US cut. Instead of Anna on the other end of the line, Marc hears a crudely distorted 'demonic' voice: "Your sleep won't bring her home, Marc. I am alive and will be here."[5] Who are we to assume this voice to belongs to? What does that statement even mean? While Żuławski's film is undoubtedly strange, it is not without logic.

Anna's subway miscarriage, which occurs over midway through Żuławski's film, is moved to the first 20 minutes of the US cut. In the director's cut, this moment is presented as a flashback of sorts—Anna is desperately trying to explain her mental state to her husband when we cut to this scene. At its conclusion we cut back to their conversation, as she explains what was happening. The scene in this instance, regardless of whether we interpret it as real or subjective, is anchored in the narrative. In the US version, it is stripped of its context entirely, ham-fistedly wedged between scenes of Marc caring for Bob at the couple's apartment, and his first encounter with Heinrich.

No doubt part of the problem is Żuławski's economical method of shooting in the first place. With just enough celluloid to capture the required shots, alternative takes and angles are few and far between. Żuławski (2000) describes his method as inspired by John Ford, who shot in such a way that a studio's ability to meddle would be limited. "Because of my poor man's cinema background, my film is already pre-cut. All my editors have always said: 'If you were to die right after shooting completed, we'd know exactly what to do, because how else could it be put together?'" (Żuławski qtd. in Wybon 2009). The US cut of *Possession* is nothing if not proof of Żuławski's logic. Any attempt to go against the grain of Żuławski's vision renders the film non-sensical.

Tuten recalls Reyre asking him to sign a release form to permit the American edit so that the film could be seen in the States. Such permissions were necessary under French copyright law which gives authors "moral rights" (*"droits moraux"*) over the integrity of their work (White & Mary 2014). It appears that this agreement granted the additional editors *carte blanche* access, not only to the film but to Żuławski's rushes and outtakes as well; the US cut contains material that does not appear in the director's cut. The most obvious instance of this is a pair of shots inserted into a much briefer version of Anna's miscarriage flashback. In what is likely a remnant of Żuławski's original intention to show multiple versions of Anna's miscarriage, we see her kneeled on the subway floor slowly raising her open hands in close-up, in each an eyeball stares blankly, recalling the imagery of the priestess's painted hands in *On the Silver Globe*.

Żuławski never watched the US cut. As far as he was concerned, Marie-Laure Reyre was swindled into a bad deal (Thrower & Bird 2003: 62). Żuławski felt that her lack of oversight likely stemmed from not understanding the film; it is difficult to put constraints that preserve the integrity of an artwork if what is integral is lost on you. The US cut of *Possession* remains a notorious and monstrous Other to its original. Today, it circulates in bootleg form, a wretched and spurned cultural curio. But the film's dramas were not limited to the United States. Across the Atlantic, an altogether different kind of storm was brewing.

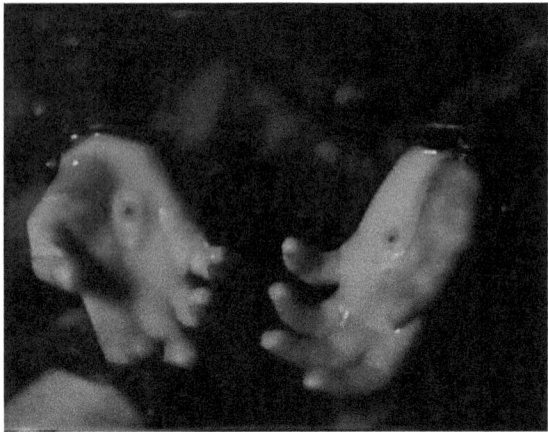

Another version of the U-Bahn sequence revealed in the US edit.

UK RELEASE AND THE VIDEO NASTIES

> This being England, an unpleasant vein of snobbery never lurks very far beneath the surface of this kind of discourse, but occasionally it rises to the surface in an unashamedly naked fashion – Julian Petley (2002: 37) on British critics and horror cinema

Possession was twice lost on English audiences. It was lost on those who did see it, deeming it an object too grotesque and strange. And then it was lost again, on those who could not see it, when upon its VHS release it would be swept up in the moral panic over violent movies and banned under obscenity laws that had previously only targeted pornography. My singling out of *Possession*'s English release is simply because it would come to cause a scandal there unrivalled in other markets. While the derision *Possession* was met with in the US is understandable given the butchering the film received in its re-edit, in England the response seemed more culturally laden. Between a long-held critical hostility towards the horror genre, a Conservative government on a moral crusade against depravity, and a tabloid press eager to fuel the flames of social anxiety over vulnerable children, *Possession* found itself embroiled in a cultural shitstorm.

Following its Cannes premiere, London Film Festival director Ken Wlaschin programmed *Possession* in LFF's Controversy section. When the film screened at the National Film Theatre on November 12th, 1981, Simon Perry of *Variety* described the response as "tepid" (1981: 7). This seemed a generous summary, however, given the venomous reviews of some. Derek Malcolm (who a few years later would become director of LFF) took a few jabs at the film in *The Guardian*, calling it one of the festival's "stumers" before suggesting Adjani's acting prize at Cannes may have been awarded out of sympathy (1981: 11). Writing for *Sight and Sound*, Tom Milne also greeted the film with vitriol, taking its very inclusion in the Festival as an affront to any expectation patrons might have for quality cinema: "Some of the selections (*Possession*, *Subway Riders*) are so abominably directed, execrably acted and pretentiously conceived that there is no excuse" (Milne & Adair 1981: 17).

Despite the negative press, *Possession* did receive a theatrical release in England, however, this too was met with disdain from reviewers. Derek Malcolm again took aim, remarking that *Possession* has "cinematography of such eccentricity and direction of such hysterical abandon that you soon start to eat your cigarette and smoke your popcorn" (1982: 11). Martyn Auty's *Monthly Film Bulletin* review was likewise punitive, criticising the film's "nonsensical narrative and preposterous psychology" while attributing it with "the most impressively repulsive special effects in years." Finally, Auty concludes: "As grand guignol, *Possession* is so lacking in humour or irony that it seems destined only for a place in some cultist list of golden turkey horror movies" (1982: 32). *Screen International*'s Majorie Bilbow was somewhat more forgiving, suggesting that the film would appeal to "film buffs with enquiring minds and strong stomachs." However, this was not without the mocking observation that Żuławski's lofty symbolism notwithstanding, "it seems one heck of a brouhaha that so many people should die just because a woman can't achieve an orgasm" (1982: 24).

I acknowledge *Possession* is abrasive—it's meant to be—but it's worth flagging this reaction in a cultural context. As Julian Petley (2002) points out, the British press has a history of showing disdain for the 'lowly' genre of horror that can be traced back to the rise of the Gothic novel, a centuries-old snobbery in relation to popular culture as degrading art's purpose as moral education. Such snobbery has grave consequences, namely the moral panic driven largely by government and the press of the 'video nasties' scandal in which *Possession* would be swept up, and which I will turn to shortly. For now, however, it is worth noting that despite the negative press, there was little to suggest that that *Possession* would be the target of censorship.

THE BBFC

> [N]o doubt if it is distributed commercially after its showing at the London Film Festival, it will be considered quite controversial. – BBFC examiner's report 20-10-81
>
> Too loud, too long & a load of hog wash but acceptable for adult X category. – BFFC examiner's report 27-1-1982

In the introduction to this book, I said that *Possession* is not a film that affords a safe, critical distance. However, a safe critical distance is precisely what members of the British Board of Film Censors were trying to adopt when assessing the suitability of Żuławski's film for local audiences. Examiners met twice to discuss *Possession* before it would screen in theatres; first in October 1981 in preparation for its debut at the London Film Festival the following month, and again in January 1982 prior to its broader theatrical release. Later, after its embroilment in the video nasties storm had blown over, examiners, now operating under the rebranded British Board of Film Classification, would meet again to discuss a suitable classification for *Possession* on video. While on all of these occasions *Possession* appears to have been met with a mixture of confusion and awe, the verdict was unanimous: the film could be accommodated intact, under an 'X', (or later equivalent '18') certificate.

At worst, the BBFC greeted the film with a bewildered respect. At best, it was regarded with enthusiasm. But even those that clearly disliked it thought it ought to be taken seriously. One examiner in 1984 was practically beaming:

> I found this film fascinating. A dissertation could be written on its presentation of sexual despair, Germanic angst, urban alienation and subliminal fears leading to political catastrophe and ultimately mass destruction...Much of our discussion after the film centred on how successfully the film brought together the wide range of issues presented and I was struck by the fact that the film's strength was the way it intelligently used Kafkaesque 'concrete metaphors' in its discourse in a fashion which

would perhaps be more accessible and immediately assimilable to German audiences than to English ones. I would like to see this film a few more times. (BFFC examiner's report 03-10-84)

Given that not once in the BBFC reports on *Possession* does an examiner suggest cuts are necessary, it seems the film was less an object for censorship than an affront to British decorum. Language was a minor concern; perhaps feeling some allegiance with the tentacle monster, one examiner observed that the "number of 'fucks' as swear words can be counted on the fingers of one hand," only to specify in the same report that the film contained "8 fucks" (BBFC examiner's report 03-10-1984). The main considerations, however, were the amount of bloody violence, and Anna's relations with the monster. It is worth pausing to consider the latter, as this presented an unusual problem for examiners. Did this image constitute bestiality? Was it eroticised? No small amount of ink is spent pondering these questions. While a point of consideration for the BBFC since 1981, the most sustained deliberation of human / monster intimacy occurs in 1984. Below are some illustrative excerpts from the 1984 examiners' reports:

Examiner 1

I can understand certain sections of the English audience being shocked by the copulation scene with the creature at 1:41, but I can find no justification for cutting this except on the grounds of manners.

Examiner 2

Scene of the copulation with the sludge at 1:41:18 and of the hysterical miscarriage in the deserted subway passage at 1:11:30 where white porridge oats seep out of her body; and of Mark face slapping Anna at 27:50 – all these make it definitely '18.' But does any of this require cutting? Despite the film's legal notoriety the bestiality shots of Anna and the sludge are hardly raunchy—her body is mostly covered by the sludge and the only explicitly vivid aspect of the sex is the thrusting motion of the tentacle…Besides the creature itself is so fantastical, and so obviously (as nothing else is) destined to turn into a man—that the full unpleasantness of bestiality, as opposed to schlock, is never conveyed.

Examiner 3

> The only controversy would seem to centre around Anna's copulation with the creature (1hr 42 min) with a suggestion for some, perhaps, of bestiality. Failure or not, the film deserves to be called serious and as this scene is not sexually graphic in a way that would normally be cut, I can see no objections to it. Without this scene, much of the film would be meaningless although some would argue this is already the case.
>
> – (BBFC examiners' reports 03-10-1984)

Ultimately, examiners agreed that Anna's tentacular tryst was incredible enough to not be harmful to viewers. That the BBFC spent so much attention considering this issue, especially in 1984, is hardly surprising given the film's infamy in Britain by this time. A woman fucking an octopus is just the kind of lurid detail that the tabloid press sought to dwell on in their moral campaign against a depraved video industry capitalising on the corruption of young minds. Moreover, only a month prior to these reports, this scene had been debated vehemently by prosecution, defence, and jurors when *Possession* was put on a publicised trial.

The 'Nasties'

> ...it has always pissed me off that the censors in the UK slapped an R18 'video nasty' something or other on it. In other words it was treated as a bit of violent porn trash.
> – Sam Neill (personal communication, March 14, 2019)

How did *Possession* go from screening in competition at the world's premiere art cinema festival to being shown in Knightsbridge Crown Court, on indictment for obscenity? There are a number of excellent resources that unpack the video nasties scandal in a far greater depth than I have scope for here,[6] however, answering this question requires a brief summary.

In the early 1980s, the British tabloids, a moral crusade spearheaded by Mary Whitehouse, and a void opened up by a new and unregulated technology—home video—would come to represent three points of another 'fundamentally vulgar structure': censorship. While all theatrical releases came under the purview of the BBFC, home videos were at the time unregulated. Until the Video Recordings Act (VRA) of 1984 which would require all video releases to be classified by the BBFC, the de facto law appealed to in the wake of the video boom was the Obscene Publications Act (OPA), which held the notoriously vague proviso that obscene works had a "tendency to deprave and corrupt" those who encounter them.

The British tabloid press was eager to fuel social anxiety over this seemingly unprecedented endemic of moral depravity. A typically histrionic *Daily Mail* editorial entitled "Rape of our children's minds" begins:

> How much longer will the Government dither and Parliament blather while our children can continue to buy sadism from the video-pusher as easily—and almost as cheaply—as they can buy fruit gums from the sweetie shop?...Thirty years ago, children went off with their Saturday sixpence to see Roy Rogers and Trigger. Now for 50p they gather in sniggering groups to view *SS Experiment Camp*. (qtd. in Barker ed. 1984: 28)

Vulnerable children were a constant image conjured by journalists, activists, and politicians in the campaign against violent videos, not least because they provided a convenient and unassailable moral icon upon which propaganda and political ideology might be draped. Unlike theatrical releases, videos were designed to be watched in the privacy of one's home and therefore the potential for children to be exposed to graphic and uncertified material was of grave concern to a society ill-equipped to control the perceived scourge of sex and sadism. However, it wasn't only children that were deemed at risk. Along with privacy, video technology presented viewers with an unprecedented level of autonomy. Much was made in hysterical press reports about viewers being able to rewind and replay ghastly scenes of violence and degradation for their own sick gratification.

With tabloid newspaper articles escalating pressure for the authorities to protect Britain from the likes of *S.S. Experiment Camp* (Garrone 1976), *Driller Killer* (Ferrara 1979), and *Cannibal Holocaust* (Deodato 1980), various law enforcement agencies as well as video distributors sought advice from the Director of Public Prosecutions (DPP) on whether offending films ought to be prosecuted, forfeited, or even destroyed (Martin 2007: 16).

The DPP would publish several lists of videos in the early 1980s, naming those which were found to be in violation of the Obscene Publications Act, and those likely to be prosecuted. The 'nasties' consisted of a hodgepodge catalogue of 69 films including everything from the truly gruesome to the innocuous but provocatively titled. *Possession* featured on this list, (one of several titles to have already been approved for theatrical release by the BBFC) suddenly deemed criminal (Petley 2011: 213-215).

Inclusion on the DPP's blacklist marked only the beginning of *Possession*'s legal trouble in the UK. The following month, on July 29th, 1983, *Possession*'s distribution company, VTC were informed that a police raid was in progress on the London offices of their distribution partner CBS. Six hundred and eighty-seven copies of *Possession* were confiscated, and sales were halted (Martin 2007: 22). Even more dramatically, on September 10th, 1984 VTC would be tried in Knightsbridge Crown Court over the distribution of *Possession* under Section 2 of the OPA.

According to John Martin's extensive coverage of the nasties scandal, the scene depicting Anna and her monstrous lover became a battleground in court. Prosecutor Kenneth Richardson warned jurors that with repeated viewing, audiences might find themselves desensitised enough to find such relations acceptable (Martin 2007: 36). The defence's case hinged in part on pointing out that the notion that anyone might be inspired to imitate such a scene was ludicrous. A *Daily Mail* article entitled "'Octopus sex' film gets OK" covered the in-court drama, quoting Mr. Richard Du Cann QC: "No-one watching this video can possibly go out and have relations with an octopus" (qtd. in Martin 1997: 211). Noting the adjacent department store, Du Cann continued: "We're not going to pop into Harrods and get an octopus on our account" (ibid.). Both Neill and Adjani would provide written statements in defence of the film (Sutherland 1984: 19). Jurors deliberated for 2 hours and 14 minutes before acquitting the film by a vote of 11 – 1 on September 12th. With this ruling, *Possession* was deemed "not obscene" (Martin 2007: 36). The following month, VTC would re-release the film, following its 18-month embargo (Martin 1997: 212).

Possession is a difficult film to define, and this lack of clarity fuels a certain discomfort when it comes to defending an aversion or appreciation. If *Possession* is just a piece of exploitative trash, with no redeeming qualities, then it can safely be quarantined as such and dismissed outright. On the other hand, if *Possession* can be shown to hold an unimpeachable pedigree as high art, then it can be sequestered from criticism to the contrary, and one's admiration is justified. Of course, like *The Devils* (Russell 1971), like *Sweet Movie* (Makavejev 1974), like *Salò* (Pasolini 1975), indeed like so many controversial predecessors, *Possession*'s tangle of art and irreverence refuse to comfortably situate it on either side of this specious boundary between high and low. It is strange to think, however, that thirty-four years after *Possession* was put on trial, *The Shape of Water* (Del Toro 2017), a $20 million USD movie about a woman who fucks with a fish man would take home four Oscars, three BAFTAs and a suite of other international cinema awards without incident. But you have to start somewhere.

FOOTNOTES

5. This voice appears again a little later in the US cut. In Żuławski's film, Marc is awoken by the telephone again, this time a male voice firmly states: "Anna is with me and she'll stay with me," before hanging up. In the US cut, it is the demonic voice we hear with an entirely new line of dialogue: "You want to see Anna with me Marc? She is here now."
6. See: Barker (ed.) (1984); Egan (2007); Martin (1997); Martin (2007); Petley (2011).

Chapter 5: 'Does Our Subject Still Wear Pink Socks?' – *Possession*'s Legacy

> It took 28 years to win over the public. And that's not a nice thought. On the other hand, it's alive. – Andrzej Żuławski (qtd. in Wybon 2009)

On a stormy night, in a tower laboratory, a mad scientist prepares his experiment for an anxious audience. "Quite a scene, isn't it? One man crazy. Three very sane spectators." Behind him is a corpse on a slab, which he elevates with a system of pulleys through a hole in the laboratory's ceiling. Cracks of lightning work their magic, the slab is lowered, the corpse's hand twitches. "It's alive!" repeats Doctor Frankenstein, first as a statement of fact, then as a maniacal chant.

Żuławski's *Possession*—itself a monster presented to a series of very sane spectators unprepared for its frenzied energy—would take a lot longer to bring to life. More than most directors, Żuławski's oeuvre has been plagued by delays and deferrals. If *The Devil* and *On the Silver Globe* were halted and hindered at the hands of Polish authorities, *Possession*'s delayed appreciation is a result of two key factors: the disastrous US edit that affected its reputation, and the ahead-of-its-time nature of the film. No doubt the forbidden-fruit status of the video nasties campaign helped to put the film, and its director, on the radar of horror fans in Western Europe and beyond. *Possession* remains Żuławski's best-known film and in the four decades since its release, the film's recognition has only continued to grow.

The efforts of writer and documentarian, Daniel Bird, have proved instrumental in bringing Żuławski's work to the attention of audiences internationally. Bird first put a spotlight on Żuławski's films with writing for Britain's horror zine *Eyeball* in collaboration with editor Stephen Thrower. These essays and reviews gave English-language readers an insight not only into *Possession* but Żuławski's wider output. Bird remains a pivotal conduit between Żuławski and audiences, securing financing for restorations and releases of Żuławski's films, as well as contributing an extensive suite of ancillary materials to home video releases.

While poorly received upon its debut, *Possession* has gradually developed a cult following. New technologies allowing for digital restorations, as well as the rise of podcasting have been pivotal in this regard. These DVDs, Blu-rays, and box sets, increasingly lavish, are indicative of the journey that *Possession* has taken since the early '80s when police were conducting raids in Britain to seize VHS copies under charges of criminal obscenity. Given the disdain for the film initially, it is remarkable to see its appreciation decades later with special releases for home viewing. In 2013, Second Sight's re-release of the film came with a wealth of new bonus features including featurettes on poster artist Basha Baranowska, the Berlin locations, and the US edit. Mondo Vision's 2014 limited edition blue velvet box set is also impressive. Here the film is lovingly restored with a 2K digital transfer approved by Żuławski, and comes with reproduced archival materials, and a digitally remastered copy of Korzyński's score. These editions in particular help to reframe Żuławski's film as a significant work of auteur cinema.

This legacy continues to grow with *Possession*'s 40th anniversary in 2021. A new 4K restoration by Le chat qui fume, supervised and approved by Céline Charrenton of TF1 Studio, promises to bring the film to the appreciation of new audiences and long-term fans. Charrenton has described a key challenge of the restoration to be capturing the coldness of 1980 Berlin through a careful colour grading process that is faithful to the quality of late '70s and early '80s cinema (Crump 2021). Thanks to this careful attention to *Possession*'s preservation, the film is seeing a new wave of theatrical and home viewing releases.

Podcasting has also provided new avenues for *Possession*'s appreciation. Kat Ellinger and Samm Deighan's *Daughters of Darkness* podcast released an exceptional four-part retrospective on Żuławski in 2016. Charting the themes and recurring imagery from Żuławski's early television work right through to his final film, *Cosmos*, this series is essential listening. Also of note is *The Projection Booth*'s three-hour consideration of *Possession* released in 2014. This episode includes interviews with the film's co-writer, Frederic Tuten as well as Daniel Bird. More recently, in 2020 *Ride the Omnibus*, *Someone Else's Movie*, and *The Evolution of Horror* podcasts have featured *Possession*, demonstrating that interest in *Possession* continues to grow, not unlike the "Lovecraftian fuck monster" gleefully described by the latter podcast's hosts.

Possession has also seen a resurgence theatrically, and this wider exposure continues to spark the appreciation of new audiences. The film's co-writer, Frederic Tuten, is amazed at the resonance it has with the younger generation. When the Anthology Film Archives in New York first requested Tuten introduce a screening of Possession (Valentine's Day screenings have been a regular occurrence since 2014) he was taken aback. "Why?" he asked, "Who knows about this film?" Assuming it would be a dead event, Tuten was stunned when he arrived to see a line of patrons stretching around the block. "It was packed! The whole place was packed...people were in the aisles. I could not believe my eyes. All young people, crazy for the film" (Tuten qtd. in Iatrou & Morgan 2019).

The Anthology Film Archives are not alone in bringing Possession and Żuławski to a wider audience. In March 2012, BAMcinématek, the Polish Cultural Institute New York, and Los Angeles's (now defunct) Cinefamily would combine forces to bring month-long retrospectives of Żuławski's work to US audiences. BAMcinématek's retrospective was entitled "Hysterical Excess: Discovering Andrzej Żuławski," a title that Żuławski expressed disdain for (Barton-Fumo 2012). I suspect Cinefamily's concurrent retrospective, "The Unbelievable Genius of Andrzej Żuławski," was more agreeable to the director. In the wake of Żuławski's passing in 2016, Cinefamily ran a week's worth of Possession screenings, before launching another retrospective of Żuławski's films. Cinefamily would collapse the following year under a wave of sexual assault allegations against one of its co-founders, however, these screenings bear mention for playing a pivotal role in bringing Possession, in its unabridged version, to the attention of North America.

Possession and Gender

While it's true that the very fact of one's corporeality makes one vulnerable in a horror film—flesh, regardless of gender, can be bitten, slashed, mutated, or otherwise violated—to be female in a horror film is so often laden with the additional obstacle of doubt; women are not only alienated from a body that no longer feels their own, but from their own experience of that body which is diminished or denied. In *Rosemary's Baby*, our heroine knows that something is very wrong with her pregnancy, but everyone around her is so ready to say 'I' for her, that she grows to mistrust her own experience. In *I Spit on Your Grave* (Zarchi 1978), *Handgun* (Garnett 1983), *Irreversible* (Noé 2002), and so many other rape-revenge movies, victims are told by their attackers what their assault means—usually some variant of 'you were asking for it.' It is of no small significance then, that Anna's experience in *Possession* refuses to be contained or explained away by those who seek to control her.

Perhaps it is not so surprising then, that in the intervening decades since *Possession*'s release, the film has gained a substantial female following. Where some might be tempted to dismiss Anna as representative of a familiar stereotype, the stock image of a hysterical woman, to many, Anna is a powerful and rare image of an unapologetically unleashed woman.

Kier-La Janisse, whose work has been instrumental in bringing attention back to *Possession*, considers the film a profound icon of self-realisation. It was *Possession* that sparked her incredible survey of neurotic women in horror, *House of Psychotic Women* (2012), with Janisse adopting Adjani's Anna as an anchoring figure through which she explores her own history and identity as "crazy." For Janisse, Anna is relatable for laying bare the neurotic tendencies that for women, unlike their "comparatively-lauded male counterpart—'the eccentric'" (2012: 8), are culturally reinforced as shameful. While she notes that some have written off Żuławski as a misogynist for his repeated representation of hysterical women, Janisse perceives Anna's madness as a radical form of liberation:

> In my house growing up, it was my voice that was a problem. I was told not to talk. As Anna struggles to talk, her whispers become growls, screams and hyperventilating. There is a freedom in this kind of self-obliteration, the collapse of propriety. (2012: 153)

Kris Shin (2019) has also found Adjani's Anna to be a relatable figure. In a personal essay for *The Daily Californian*, Shin reflects on her enduring love of *Possession*. The U-Bahn scene is of particular significance, because like Janisse, and so many women, Shin has been told to stifle and subjugate her emotions. In Anna, she discovered the catharsis of witnessing a woman defiantly losing her shit. For Shin, this moment also captured her desire to shed a body that comes steeped in a cultural tendency to diminish women by aligning their worth to their bodies:

My affecting experience of the subway scene is shaped by the historical weight of gendered violence, the expectations and forms of domination that constrict the historical and political category of women, reducing and binding them to bodies. The body is a burden, the locus of associations I have no control over.

Thus, I disassociate, disavow and disconnect from mine. (Shin 2019)

Additionally, Canadian film critic, Justine Peres Smith has been vocal about *Possession*'s resonance with women, asserting in 2014 that, "A man who has never seen Żuławski's *Possession* does not truly understand what it is to be a woman." These words have stuck with me since I first read them, pointing towards the film's ability to articulate something about female experience that I knew was there but hadn't quite put my finger on. Smith has since elaborated on *Possession*'s significance for her personally:

> While the film takes a largely male point of view, it nonetheless stood out for me as a portrait of womanhood that I never saw expressed. It was not respectable, it was not contained… it was larger than life, literally possessed. It explored the monstrosity of womanhood in a way that didn't feel punitive in the way American slashers were, it was empathetic to the alienation experienced by many women towards their bodies. To this day, I think there are so few movies that showcase the 'unruliness' of femininity in a way that feels so ruthless in its emotional realism, without also purely showcasing that same unruliness as purely monstrous. (J. Smith, personal communication, Oct 23, 2020)

Anna's struggles with communication, identity, and her own corporeality continue to resonate with female audiences. Her inability to express herself, her physical expulsion of emotions that resist the coherence of language, is in itself a powerful statement of expression. If one feels enculturated to be proper, quiet, even timid, to see oneself through the gaze of men, then bearing witness to the violent and unbridled collapse of such expectations feels revolutionary.

To note that *Possession* resonates strongly with female audiences, is not to say that its appreciation is limited to women. As Alexandra Heller-Nicholas (2016a) notes, because Anna is both a mother and desiring woman, there is a tendency to perceive her struggle as uniquely female, yet the film's emotional honesty continues to resonate in ways that are not gendered. Reflecting on the impact of *Possession*, director Buddy Giovinazzo has felt both attached to the suffering of Marc, but also sees the couple's dynamic as one that is not confined to gender:

> The helplessness of Sam Neill just broke my heart. I've sort of been in that situation…So I guess it really just touched me in such an emotional, personal way that when it's over and there's nothing you can do…Interestingly enough, [*The Bitter Tears of*] *Petra Von Kant* is almost the exact same situation. Carstensen is losing her lover and she's so crazy in love with her, and there's nothing she can do…It transcends gender. To me, [*The Bitter Tears of Petra Von Kant* is] not a lesbian love story, it's a love story, because it's so universal. And again, I was Margit Carstensen in my first marriage, so I look at this and it touches me in a way that *Possession* touches me. (personal communication, September 12, 2020)

In a similar way, Madeline Sims-Fewer, co-director and star of *Violation* (2020) has reflected on her relationship to *Possession*, noting that her connection to it has changed over time.

> I think when I first watched it I really, really related to Sam Neill and then now- just because of the way that I've changed and different perspectives that I have on life, I relate to Adjani more and just this idea that she, even though she loves him, she has to escape, but then in escaping she then recreates the same thing again, she kind of is reaching for something else but then finds out that it's still him. (qtd. in Wilner 2020)

Possession's amorphous style lends itself to multiple readings. While it certainly speaks to many women, myself included, I think what also resonates with viewers is the film's approach to the very human experience of anguish. Miscommunication, the inability to relate to one another, and the inherent suffering that is part of deteriorating connections between those who love one another is, of course, not limited to one's gendered experience.

Legacy and Influence

In February of 2016, aged 75, Andrzej Żuławski succumbed to cancer. The same year, Amat Escalante's Mexican-Euro co-production, *The Untamed* (2016) ran the festival circuit. Żuławski is thanked in the end credits and *The Untamed* is a fitting sendoff—it too is about a woman who fucks with an octopus. *Possession*'s influence is unmistakable; Escalante's creature—which sends those who encounter it into an otherworldly sexual ecstasy—bears a striking resemblance to Anna's monster, though it is modern CGI effects rather than film stock and glue that render its tentacles tumescent and slick.

Possession's legacy has been slow to emerge, yet it has left an indelible mark on cinema, not least it in its pioneering status. While certainly not the first extreme film to grace the festival circuit, as Hobbs (2018: 191) notes, "Żuławski's combination of visual experimentation and gory special effects frames *Possession* as a text of some importance to the genealogy of extreme art film." The mixing of "low" gore, sex, or otherwise transgressive content with the "high" of art film festivals has grown increasingly common in the decades since. The late '90s and early '00s delivered what is now known as the New French Extremity, with boundary-pushing auteurs including Catherine Breillat, Gaspar Noé, and Claire Denis. Beyond France, we have seen the provocations of Lars von Trier, Nicolas Winding Refn, Park Chan-wook, Yorgos Lanthimos, and Sandra Wollner to name just a few.

The film has also influenced and inspired filmmakers in more direct ways. Buddy Giovinazzo's contribution to *The Theatre Bizarre* (2011), a horror anthology film inspired by Grand Guignol theatre pays homage to *Possession*. Like *Possession*, Giovinazzo's short, *I Love You*, literalises the horror of a failed marriage, and the desperate and destructive urge to possess the other. Axel (André Hennicke) awakens hung over on his bathroom floor with an injured hand from an incident he does not remember. From here, *I Love You*'s elliptical narrative appears to reveal the events that led up to this moment in which his wife, Mo (Suzan Anbeh) returns to their Berlin apartment to terminate the relationship once and for all. Żuławski's influence can be felt throughout; reminiscent lines of dialogue, shot compositions, and toxic relationship dynamics place *I Love You* in conversation with *Possession*. At the same time, Giovinazzo satisfyingly wrings the changes—unlike Anna, Mo is piercingly articulate about her needs and Axel's inability to fulfil them.

I Love You *(Giovinazzo 2011)* © Severin Films/Metaluna Productions/Nightscape Entertainment

Describing the film's bloody climax, Giovinazzo laughs: "Well the last shot is… I can't even say it's a tribute – I stole it. I was just so inspired" (personal communication, September 12, 2020).

This direct citation of *Possession*'s imagery is also evident in Ringan Ledwidge's music video for Massive Attack's "Voodoo in my Blood," which combines influences from Żuławski's film, and Don Coscarelli's *Phantasm* (1979). In explicit reference to *Possession*'s U-Bahn sequence, Ledwidge's film follows Rosmund Pike in a blue dress, entering an empty subway tunnel where is she is both hypnotised and tormented by a sinister mechanical orb. Pike's physicality and expression recall Adjani's, as she is compelled and contorted into a manic dance.

The U-Bahn sequence also serves as the inspiration for a 2004 short film by art / fashion duo Lily Ludlow and Marcella Mullins. The pair pay homage to Żuławski's imagery and Korzyński's score in something like a runway show turned transgressive horror. Cutting between five women in the role of Anna (including Chloë Sevigny) the film recreates Adjani's subway meltdown in graphic detail.

In so many ways, Adjani's groundbreaking performance in *Possession* remains influential. Director of *Raw* (2016), Julia Ducournau describes having her performers watch Żuławski's film in preparation for shooting the coming-of-age body horror. In *Raw*, Justine (Garance Marrilier) joins her older sister at university to follow in the family

Hagazussa *(Feigelfeld 2017)* © *Deutsche Film und Fernsehakademie Berlin.*

"Voodoo in My Blood" *(Ledwidge 2016)* © *Massive Attack/Rattling Stick*

tradition of veterinary science, when a hazing ritual that requires her to break her strict vegetarian diet inadvertently unleashes a cannibalistic bloodlust. Ducournau explains that Adjani's performance was essential viewing: "Garance had to abandon herself in many scenes and to be completely not conscious of her body at all, and I told her if you want to see what it is not to be conscious anymore as an actress watch this; this is pure art" (qtd. in Heller-Nicholas 2016b).

Other filmmakers have seen Adjani's performance as educative in capturing a loss of sanity. Both Lukas Feigelfeld and Gaspar Noé have taken their cues from *Possession* in depicting a drug-fuelled psychological meltdown albeit in differing contexts. Feigelfeld's 2017 film *Hagazussa* is indebted to Żuławski and Adjani. Dark and atmospheric,

Hagazussa is set in the fifteenth-century Alps, where unforgiving winters and sprawling fairytale forests furnish its protagonist's psychological deterioration. After enduring the cruelty and assaults born of pagan superstition, Albrun (Aleksandra Cwen) suffers a psychotic reaction to wild mushrooms, during which she kills and eats her child. Violently ill, Albrun seizes and screams in a posture that mirrors Adjani's in the subway.

More recently, Gaspar Noé's *Climax* (2018) also made its homage to *Possession* overt. In a prologue sequence, we watch casting interviews of dancers applying to join a troupe. These fragmented moments are relayed on an old television set framed with VHS tapes including *Possession*, *Suspiria*, and Kenneth Anger's *The Inauguration of the Pleasure Dome* (1954) amongst several others. The bulk of the film thereafter charts the deteriorating sanity of these dancers after someone spikes the sangria at a post-rehearsal party with LSD. Noé's combination of dance and psychedelic whodunnit horror provides many opportunities to exploit frenetic performance. Memorably, Sophia Boutella's character, Selva, channels Adjani's subway meltdown in an acid-fuelled paranoid freak-out.

That Adjani's performance in *Possession* is held up as acting craft to be emulated is both inevitable given its uniqueness, and uncomfortable given the mythology that surrounds its creation. It is, undoubtedly, a tremendous achievement which ought to be acknowledged, but hearing the personal cost at which it came cannot help but temper this appreciation. This tension borne of Żuławski the artist, and the impact of the art that he left in his wake is broached in the film *Bird Talk*.

BIRD TALK (XAWERY ŻUŁAWSKI 2019)

Before he died, Żuławski gifted his son, Xawery, a screenplay. Xawery was already an established filmmaker in his own right, though perhaps "gifted" is the wrong word. To hand over an unfinished work, presumably with the hope your legacy might endure must carry a weight, if not a burden, that gifts don't have. It was the framework of what would become *Bird Talk*. The film follows a bunch of misfit creatives attempting survive in contemporary Warsaw where one regime of oppression has merely been replaced by another; the communist shackles that Żuławski critiqued in so many of his films are here superseded by a virulent Polish nationalism.

Bird Talk is a stirring piece and one immediately recognises Xawery's homage to his father's work in the frenetic energy of the dialogue, themes of love and death, the intellectualised play with language and liberal references to Tolstoy. Moreover, the late Żuławski's key crew members have reprised their roles; Jaroszewicz operates the camera, Korzyński scores. Xawery's continuation of his father's artistic legacy is made more personal, however, with gestures both benign and acerbic. In the former category, the film is interspersed with gratifying references to his father's prior films. In the latter, some nimble though barbed jabs are struck at Andrzej with frank observation.

Late in the film, fiction and reality blur, when high school teacher Marian (Sebastian Fabijanski) returns to his aging director father's home with one of his former pupils, Aja (Katarzyna Chojnacka), a sixteen-year-old aspiring filmmaker in tow. The camera traces over a room cluttered with archival objects—framed posters of Żuławski's films, festival awards, and on-set photographs of a young Żuławski at work. Daniel Olbrychski plays Mr. Gustaw, the father / director, a Żuławski avatar who has been banned from filmmaking. "I only made one film in English, and I'm still living off it, sort of." Gustaw tells the girl, adding with an air of lechery: "Want me to show you?"

On a television screen a maniacal Adjani clutches her bag grinning wide and enters the filthy U-Bahn. Aja stares wide-eyed and upset at Anna who begins to seize and throw. Bursting downstairs, distraught, Aja tells Marian his father's films are "horrible." She prefers beautiful films. She prefers *Dances with Wolves*. The nod is a funny one, but it also speaks to the power *Possession*, and particularly Adjani's performance holds. The film's impact has not dissipated over time; with the exception of Berlin's Cold War landscape, it feels as immediate as ever. Still distressing, *Possession* is a film that grips and disturbs.

POSSESSION AND 'THE HORROR'

It's a curious feeling to come towards the end of a book about *Possession* as a great horror film, only to find yourself simultaneously questioning just how much of a horror film it actually is. I said in Chapter 1 that *Possession* is hardly a "straight horror film," and by this I mean it is also so many other things. Perhaps, as Lindsay Hallam argues, such distinctions as to what is and is not "horror" are reductive anyway; imposing a narrow view takes away from the genre's diversity and complexity, reducing it to a misguided perception that horror is no more than "a cheap rollercoaster ride with a scant regard for narrative and a bloodthirsty attitude" (Hallam 2018: 95). Of course, some horror films are a formulaic exercise in eliciting shock and disgust, and there is great pleasure to be found in stepping onto the rollercoaster. But there are also those like *Possession*, like *Fire Walk With Me* (Lynch 1992), like *Antichrist* to name just a few, that employ horror to examine strands of the labyrinthine spectrum of human experience.

Maybe it is better to say that in pitching the ordinary at such a key that it becomes horrific to us, *Possession* pushes the boundaries on what we perceive as horror. While stylistically disparate, David Lynch's *Fire Walk With Me* is a good point of comparison in this regard. As Hallam notes of Lynch's articulation of trauma of incest, "Lynch places the ultimate horror not in some fantastical or outwardly Gothic ominous setting, but in a middle-class home, at the divided heart of the nuclear family unit" (2018: 76). Likewise, while *Possession* is mysterious, its horror is not abstract or supernatural. It is in the fabric of a family, growing apart in ways that they are unable to express that Żuławski locates what is truly horrific.

For Giovinazzo, it is *Possession*'s realism and relatability that strikes a chord. "I think it brought horror onto a higher level," he reflects:

> What it does to horror is it brings a first rate, first class drama in a political setting as a horror film into the genre because most horror films aren't about anything. People go to a house, it's possessed. There are demons. [*Possession*] is about something, asides from the monster it's a completely believable story in every way…That's what I think the legacy is to show that horror is on a higher level sometimes, horror reflects reality. I'm much more horrified by the real monsters than the demons and the ghosts. In all my films the monsters are real. And that's what *Possession* is to me.
> (B. Giovinazzo, personal communication, September 12, 2020)

As mentioned in Chapter 1, Żuławski has described using genre as a "mask" in order to advance social commentary. While this was in part out of necessity—one could not simply expect the socio-political critiques of films like *The Devil* and *On the Silver Globe* to go unnoticed by Polish authorities without some form of disguise—with *Possession*, genre is more revelatory. The political critique of communism is present, of course, though here it is not so much hidden as it is available as one of several concurrent layers with which to make sense of the film's mysteries. Likewise, genre is recruited in *Possession* not to hide, but to reveal the monstrosity at the essence of human relationships and conflict. I think Bird (qtd. in Deighan 2016) explains this tension between genre and and Żuławski's project best, noting that, "[Żuławski] was interested in the heart of darkness… He disliked horror as a genre, but was obviously very much interested in 'the horror, the horror.'"

"The horror! The horror!" – the enigmatic last words of Mr. Kurtz in Conrad's *Heart of Darkness* are willfully ambiguous in their referent, and in their opacity, they carry meaning that stretches beyond the immediate context of their utterance. Variously interpreted as the horror of Kurtz's physical and mental deterioration, the horror perpetrated by colonialism, the horror of the human soul, the horror of the abyss staring back, and so on, ad infinitum, one can see the parallels with the varied tendrils of Żuławski's *Possession*.

One of the pleasures in writing this book has been speaking with, and reading accounts of people who, like myself, have been carrying *Possession* around with them for years. Some have found solace in its relevance to their own experiences, others have been disturbed by it for exactly the same reason. Usually, it's a mixture of these emotions. My reading of Żuławski's film is but one among many made available by a filmmaker whose vision was deeply personal, intentionally nebulous, but at the same time profoundly human. That the film is so open to manifold layers of interpretation is undoubtedly part of its hold on audiences even decades after its release.

'I WANTED TO SHOW IT TO YOU. IT IS FINISHED NOW'

> I was walking the streets I remember, it was raining and I said look, the beauty of the stories that we are telling our children is the moral at the end. That is to say that there is always something fantastic by the end of the story. So they walk along the pavement and they go into the house… this is the first floor, this is the kitchen, blah blah, but what's in the attic? And I was thinking, okay, in my little story what attic does it really have? If I go up the stairs out of the realistic realm and into the fantasy, the

science fiction, what is the fairy tale? What is the bad fairy tale at the end? So I went to the attic and I found a monster. – Andrzej Żuławski (qtd. in Barton-Fumo 2012)

It is telling that Żuławski uses the word "moral" as interchangeable with "fantastic" here. Consider for a moment, some horrifying moments from children's stories, like when Bluebeard's wife, overwhelmed by curiosity in his absence, unlocks the one room she is forbidden to enter only to discover the terrible fate of his previous partners. Or the horror when the man in *The Velvet Ribbon* who, frustrated by his wife's refusal to tell him why she wears a ribbon around her neck, finally cuts it loose causing her head to fall to the floor. Where we might take the monster in the attic as cautionary, Żuławski is more concerned with affect. It is the impression of such moments, rather than the 'message' that matters. Elsewhere he has described his intention to make films that are about morality, but which do not moralise, and this is an important distinction. For Żuławski, to preach to an audience is not the role of cinema, rather he trusts that his audience is intelligent enough to take away what they need from a film. "My films are open-ended, I hope...You have to know by the end what's your answer to what you see" (Żuławski 2000).

Long before I began writing this book, I had decided that venturing up *Possession*'s winding staircase was something I wanted to do before I died. I didn't really entertain the notion that this would be possible—I had no idea where it was, one of thousands of anonymous staircases in Berlin. It was Kier-La Janisse's intrepid travels before me that made it possible. Published in 2014, Janisse's 'The Psychotronic Tourist: *Possession*' detailed the film's locations with present day images for comparison. Thanks to Janisse, I had a map.

In the spring of 2019, I was *en route* to Berlin, map in hand. Over the next three weeks, I would set out from my rented apartment in Kreuzberg and trek to and fro across the city. A leafy stroll from Marc and Anna's apartment block on Bernauerstraße deposited me at Bob's school. I sat in on a service at the church where Anna has the encounter with Christ crucified, preceding her subway miscarriage. A comparatively sedate coffee at Café Einstein, mirror panels still adorning the walls though it is now leather that lines the seats. A toast to Heinrich at Restaurant Stiege, before visiting Anna's clandestine apartment on Sebastianstraße just a few blocks away; the façade looks the same except for the fact it is no longer hugged by the Wall. In three quarters of an hour, you can commute to Grunewald station, and then walk the additional fifteen minutes through the upmarket mansion-adorned streets to Margie's house. And so on.

If ever there was a totemic symbol that represented the sway *Possession* held over me, however, it was the winding staircase of the Palais on Joseph-Haydn Strasse. Throughout this book, I've pitched it as the metaphorical heart of *Possession*—indicative of an aesthetic patterning that provides a way into this unwieldy film. It is a symbolic passage between Heaven and Earth, scaled by those who suffer. It is framework that gives shape to Żuławski's formal logic, the winding, evolution that is the same but different. But seeing it firsthand made real to me its status as a literal, physical structure. The varnished timber handrail, the ornate cast-iron balustrade, the serpentine contours advancing towards the grand skylight some twenty meters above.

Do I understand, *Possession*? Better, yes. Completely, no; it is not a mystery to be solved. To return to the opening of this book—like the winding staircase, here we are at the same place but somehow different. If you step over the threshold, *Possession*, for better or worse, is a film you cannot shake off. My own inability to shake the film led me to write this book. It also took me across the world to find out what I could about how it came to be. I hope I never shake it. I did not fall in love with a *message*, I fell in love with an impression, mysterious and endlessly repeatable.

BIBLIOGRAPHY

Adjani, I. (1981) Interviewed by Jean-Claude Carrière and Eve Ruggieri. [online]. https://www.youtube.com/watch?v=jjkZ7J5LqWo&t=2s (Accessed 14 Jan. 2019).

'A Film by Andre Żuławski: Now in Preproduction' (1979) *Variety* (295), 190 [Pre-production advertisement] Oliane Productions.

Auty, M. (1982) 'Possession', *The Monthly Film Bulletin*, (vol. 49 no. 576), 31-32.

Baroncelli, J. (1981, May 27) '*Possession*, d'Andrzej Żuławski: Le royaume du mal'. *Le Monde* [online] https://www.lemonde.fr/archives/article/1981/05/27/possession-d-andrzej-Żuławski-le-royaume-du-mal_3042270_1819218.html (Accessed 4 Mar. 2019).

Barker, M. (ed.) (1984) *The Video Nasties: Freedom and Censorship in the Media*. London: Pluto Press.

Barton-Fumo, M. (2012, March 6). 'Interview: Andrzej Żuławski', *Film Comment* [online] https://www.filmcomment.com/blog/film-comment-interview-andrzej-Żuławski/ (Accessed 20 Dec. 2020).

Bataille, G. (1986) *Erotism: Death & Sensuality*. Trans. M. Dalwood. San Francisco: City Lights.

BBFC (1981, October 20). Possession. [Examiner's Report]. BBFC archives, London, England.

BBFC (1982, January 27). Possession. [Examiner's Report]. BBFC archives, London, England.

BBFC (1984, October 3). Possession. [Examiner's Report]. BBFC archives, London, England.

Bilbow, M. (1982) 'Possession', *Screen International*, (350), 24.

Bird, D. (1998) 'Żuławski and the Devil' in D. Bird (ed.) *Żuławski*. Keele: Why say "I love you" when one can say "an egg"?, n.p.

Bird, D. (2003a) 'Żuławski and Polish Cinema', In S. Thrower (ed.), *Eyeball Compendium*. Surrey: FAB Press, 147-150.

Bird, D. (2003b) 'Żuławski's Possession', In S. Thrower (ed.), *Eyeball Compendium*. Surrey: FAB Press, 367-374.

Bird, D. (dir.) (2009a) *The Other Side of the Wall: The Making of Possession*. [Film] Bildstörung.

Bird, D. (2009b) 'God Figured as a Public Whore Gone Crazy: Notes on Andrzej Żuławski's Possession (1981)', in Mondo Vision (2014) *Possession* [Blu-ray box set] http://www.mondo-vision.com/possessionle.php

Bird, D. (2012) 'Re-Possession: An Appraisal by Daniel Bird', in *Andrzej Korzynski's Music Score for Andrzej Żuławski's Motion Picture Possession* [vinyl record sleeve] Finders Keepers. https://www.finderskeepersrecords.com/shop/andrzej-korzynski-possession/

Bird, D. (2021) 'My Dinner with Andrzej', *Metrograph* [online] https://metrograph.com/my-dinner-with-andrzej/ (Accessed 29 Oct. 2021).

Blake, William (1799-1806 circa) *Jacob's Ladder* [drawing]. London: The British Museum.

Bonitzer, P. (1981) '*Possession*: Inferno', *Cahiers du Cinéma*, (326), 50-51.

Bonitzer, P. & Toubiana, S. (1981) 'Entretien avec Andrzej Żuławski', *Cahiers du Cinéma*, (326), 41-49.

Borkowski, J. (1981) 'Le dernier film d'Andrzej Żuławski: Possession', *L'Avant-Scène Cinéma*, (268), 7.

Canby, V. (1983, October 28) 'Possession: Blood and Horror with Isabelle Adjani', *New York Times*, C.10.

Carre, M. (1989) 'Possession (1981)', *Samhain*, (18), 19-20.

Cavell, S. (2003) *Pursuits of Happiness: The Hollywood Comedy of Remarriage*. Massachusetts: Harvard University Press.

Climacus, J. (1982) *The Ladder of Divine Ascent*. New York: Paulist Press.

Corliss, R. (1981) 'Richard Corliss from Cannes', *Film Comment*, (Sept/Oct), 4-6.

Crawley, T. (1982) 'Possession', *Starburst Magazine*, (44), 17-18.

Crump, A. (2021) '40 Years Later, Possession is Recut, Restored and Ready for its Horror Audience', *Paste* [online] https://www.pastemagazine.com/movies/possession-4k-anniversary/ (Accessed 1 Nov. 2021).

Deighan, S. (2016) 'An Interview with Daniel Bird', *Diabolique Magazine* [online] https://diaboliquemagazine.com/interview-daniel-bird/ (Accessed 18 Mar. 2019).

Denny, A. (2016) 'The Cult Inspirations Behind Massive Attack's New Video', *Dazed* [online] https://www.dazeddigital.com/music/article/30051/1/the-cult-inspirations-behind-massive-attack-s-new-video (Accessed 17 Nov. 2020).

d'Estais, J. (2018) *Possession d'Andrzej Żuławski: Tentatives d'exorcisme*. Aix-en-Provence: Rouge Profond.

Egan, K. (2007) *Trash or Treasure?: Censorship and the Changing Meanings of the Video Nasties*. Manchester: Manchester University Press.

Ellinger, K. & Deighan, S. (2016) 'I Can't be Close to you Without Suffering: The Cinema of Andrzej Żuławski', *Daughters of Darkness*, (4-7), [Audio podcast episodes] https://diaboliquemagazine.com/the-cinema-of-andrzej-Żuławski-part-1/

Fortier, A. (1981) 'Possession', *Séquences: La revue de cinéma*, (106), 39-42.

French, P. (1981, May 31) 'Poland's First Prize', *The Observer*, 31.

Gelb, N. (1986) *The Berlin Wall: Kennedy, Khrushchev, and a Showdown in the Heart of Europe*. New York: Times Books.

Goddard, M. (2012) 'The Impossible Polish New Wave and its Accursed Émigré Auteurs: Borowczyk, Polański, Skolimowski, and Żuławski' in A. Imre (ed.) *A Companion to Eastern European Cinemas*. Chichester: Wiley-Blackwell, 291-310.

Goddard, M. (2014) 'Beyond Polish Moral Realism: The Subversive Cinema of Andrzej Żuławski' in E. Mazierska and M. Goddard (eds.) *Polish Cinema in a Transnational Context*. Rochester: University of Rochester Press, 236-257.

Grotowski, J. (2002) *Towards a Poor Theatre*. New York: Routledge.

Guigou, J. (dir.) (2014) 'Video Interview with Translator Eric Veux' in Mondo Vision (2014) *Possession* [Blu-ray box set] http://www.mondo-vision.com/possessionle.php

Hallam, Lindsay (2018) *Twin Peaks: Fire Walk With Me*. Leighton Buzzard: Auteur.

Hawkins, J. (1999) 'Sleaze Mania, Euro-Trash, and High Art: The Place of European Art Films in American Low Culture', *Film Quarterly*, (53.2), 14-29.

Heller-Nicholas, A. (2016a) 'Andrzej Żuławski and the Powerlessness of Language', *Overland* [online] https://overland.org.au/2016/02/andrzej-Żuławski-and-the-powerlessness-of-language/ (Accessed 21 Nov. 2020).

Heller-Nicholas, A. (2016b, November 25) 'In person interview with Julia Ducournau', Monsterfest (Lido Cinema, Hawthorne, Melbourne, Australia). Thanks to Alexandra Heller-Nicholas for access to the recording of the full, unpublished interview (Heller-Nicholas also extends thanks to Kier-La Janisse for organising the interview).

Hobbs, S. (2018) *Cultivating Extreme Art Cinema: Text, Paratext and Home Video Culture*. Edinburgh: Edinburgh University Press.

Hoberman, J. (2012) 'Food, Politics and Sex, Brought to a Boil' *New York Times* [online] https://www.nytimes.com/2012/03/04/movies/hysterical-excess-andrzej-Żuławski-films-at-bamcinematek.html (Accessed 21 Nov. 2020).

Insdorf, A. (1981) 'Highlights of the Cannes Film Festival', *Cineaste* (vol. 11 no. 3), 27-29, 41.

Janisse, K. (2012) *House of Psychotic Women: An Autobiographical Topography of Female Neurosis in Horror and Exploitation Films*. Surrey: FAB Press.

Janisse, K. (2014) 'The Psychotronic Tourist: *Possession* (1981)', *Spectacular Optical* [online] http://www.spectacularoptical.ca/2014/02/the-psychotronic-tourist-possession-1981/ (Accessed 3 Oct. 2018).

Klifa, T. & Lavoignat, J. (2002) 'Isabelle Adjani L'Indomptable', *Studio*, (176), 64-77.

Laster, D. (2016) *Grotowski's Bridge Made of Memory: Embodied Memory, Witnessing and Transmission in Grotowski Work*. Calcutta: Seagull Books.

Iatrou & Morgan. (2019, September 25) *Frederic Tuten on Possession* [Video] https://www.youtube.com/watch?v=z7flCN6j0_Y&t=7s&fbclid=IwAR000fXIuTl6PKVoP4rPnYy-0qzCrH4atQjg8tWI00u5dNODstbFMOp7E6U

Ludlow, L. & Mullins, M. (dir.) (2004, September 5). *Possession* [Video] https://marcjwolf.com/film-music/possession/

Malcolm, D. (1981, November 19) 'All Hands Clapping: Derek Malcolm on London Film Festival Highlights', *The Guardian*, 11.

Malcolm, D. (1982, June 24) 'No Sex Please...' *The Guardian*, 11.

Martin, J. (1997) *The Seduction of the Gullible: The Curious History of the British "Video Nasty" Phenomenon*. Nottingham: Procrustes Press.

Martin, J. (2007) *Seduction of the Gullible: The Truth Behind the Video Nasty Scandal*. Liskeard: Stray Cat.

Martin, R.H. (1985) 'Carlo Rambaldi: The Father of E.T. Begats a Werewolf!', *Fangoria*, (43), 43-46.

Mazierska, E. (2007). *Polish Postcommunist Cinema: From Pavement Level*. Oxford: Peter Lang.

Milne, T. & Adair, G. (1981) 'London 25'. *Sight and Sound*, (51.1), 16-19.

Milton, J. (2014) *Paradise Lost*. London: Penguin.

Mishałek, B. & Turaj, F. (1988) *The Modern Cinema of Poland*. Bloomington: Indiana University Press.

Niogret, H. (1981) 'Les doubles concertants (possession)', *Positif*, (no. 244-245), 114-115.

Oliane Productions (1979, May 9) 'A Film by Andre Żuławski: Now in Preproduction' [Pre-production advertisement] in *Variety* (vol. 295 iss. 1), 190.

Oliane Productions (1980, May 28) 'Possession' [Pre-production advertisement] in Variety (vol. 299 iss. 4), 33.

Perry, S. (1981, December 2) 'Crowds Flock, Parties Pour', *Variety* (vol. 305 iss. 5), 7.

Petley, J. (2002) '"A Crude Sort of Entertainment for a Crude Sort of Audience": The British Critics and Horror Cinema' in S. Chibnall and J. Petley (eds) *British Horror Cinema*. London: Routledge, 23-41.

Petley, J. (2011) *Film and Video Censorship in Modern Britain*. Edinburgh: Edinburgh University Press.

Roud, R. (1981, May 28) 'Richard Roud Reports on the Festival Prizewinners at Cannes', *The Guardian*, 8.

Sanborn, K. (1983) *Super-8/Berlin: The Architecture of Division*. Buffalo: Hallwalls.

Schneidre, D. (2017) *Trois verres de vodka*. Paris: JC Lattès.

Shin, K. (2019) 'The Nightmare of Corporeality in Andrzej Żuławski's Possession:

A Personal Essay', *The Daily Californian: Weekender* [online] https://www.dailycal.org/2019/10/25/the-nightmare-of-corporeality-in-andrzej-Żuławskis-possession-a-personal-essay/ (Accessed 5 Jan. 2021).

Sineux, M. (1981) 'Yaourt-session (possession)', *Positif* (no. 244-245), 116.

Skoczen, J. (dir.) (2000) *Żuławski on Żuławski*. [Film] Canal+ Polska, Studio Filmowe Everest.

Slowiak, J. & Cuesta, J. (2018) *Jerzy Grotowski*. New York: Routledge.

Smith, J. (@redroomrantings). "A man who has never seen Żuławski's *Possession* does not truly understand what it is to be a woman." 23 June 2014. [Tweet] https://twitter.com/redroomrantings/status/480839450490986496 (Accessed 21 Nov. 2020).

Sutherland, A. (1984, September 22) 'Collins Criticises DPP', *Screen International*, 19, 26.

Tessier, M. (1981a) 'Possession', *Image et son – La revue du cinéma*, (361), 19-22.

Tessier, M. (1981b) 'Possession d'Andrzej Żuławski', *Lumière du cinéma* (5).

The Ferroni Brigade (2012) 'Beginnings are Useless: A Conversation with Andrzej Żuławski', *Notebook* [online] https://mubi.com/notebook/posts/beginnings-are-useless-a-conversation-with-andrzej-Żuławski (Accessed 7 Mar. 2019).

Thompson, D. (2007) 'On the Silver Globe', *Sight and Sound*, (17.10), 89-90.

Thrower, S. & Bird, D. (2003) 'Cinema Superactivity: Andrzej Żuławski interviewed by Stephen Thrower & Daniel Bird' in S. Thrower (ed.), *Eyeball Compendium*. Surrey: FAB Press, 61-71.

White, M. & Mary, R. (2014) 'Possession (1981)', *The Projection Booth*, (167), [Audio podcast episode] https://www.projectionboothpodcast.com/2014/05/episode-167-possession.html

Williams, L. (1989) *Hard Core: Power, Pleasure and the "Frenzy of the Visible"*. Berkeley: University of California Press.

Wilner, N. (2020, September 11) 'Madeline Sims-Fewer on Possession', Someone Else's Movie, [Audio podcast episode] https://www.someoneelsesmovie.com/2020/09/11/madeleine-sims-fewer-on-possession/

Wybon, J. (dir.) (2009) 'Andrzej Żuławski Interview', in Mondo Vision (2014) *Possession* [Blu-ray box set] http://www.mondo-vision.com/possessionle.php

Żuławski, A. (dir.). (2000) *Possession* [Director's Commentary] Anchor Bay.

Devil's Advocates

"Auteur Publishing's new Devil's Advocates critiques on individual titles offer bracingly fresh perspectives from passionate writers. The series will perfectly complement the BFI archive volumes." Christopher Fowler, Independent on Sunday

DAUGHTERS OF DARKNESS – KAT ELLINGER

Daughters of Darkness (1971) is a vampire film like no other. Heralded as psychological high-Gothic cinema, loved for its art-house and erotic flavors, Harry Kümel's 1971 cult classic is unwrapped in intricate detail by writer Kat Ellinger to unravel the many mysteries surrounding just what makes it so appealing.

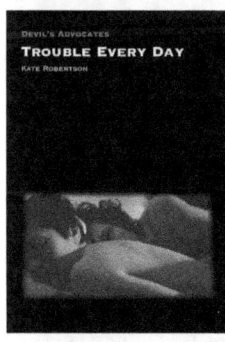

TROUBLE EVERY DAY – KATE ROBERTSON

Transgressive both in its narrative and in its filmmaking, Trouble Every Day (2001) envisions the monster inside, unspeakable urges and an overwhelming need for complete incorporation. Focusing on close textual analysis, this book delves into the surfeit of visual, literary, and non-fiction references that shape the film while thwarting attempts to firmly situate it.

TWIN PEAKS: FIRE WALK WITH ME – LINDSAY HALLAM

Lindsay Hallam argues that the horror genre aids David Lynch's purpose in presenting the protagonist Laura Palmer's subjective experience leading to her death, the incorporation of horror tropes leading to a more accurate representation of a victim's suffering and confusion.

www.ingramcontent.com/pod-product-compliance
Lightning Source LLC
Chambersburg PA
CBHW051543230426
43669CB00015B/2710